FOURTEEN PLUS

FOURTEEN PLUS
HOMESTEADING IN NEBRASKA'S SANDHILLS
1911-1949

BY DON LINEBACK

GOLDEN QUILL PRESS
Manchester Center, Vermont

GOLDEN QUILL PRESS
Manchester Center, Vermont

Library of Congress
Card Catalog Number 96-75884

I.S.B.N.
0-8233-0509-0

Printed in the United States of America

DEDICATION

Fourteen Plus is dedicated to Mom and Dad and my brothers and sisters who are deceased.

Paul Lineback (1890-1969)
Ocia (Dwiggins) Lineback (1893-1973)
Helen (Lineback) Cook (1912-1961)
Homer Lineback (1913-1987)
Paul Lineback, Jr. (1917-1994)
Rodney Lineback (1919-1982)
Catherine (Lineback) Halkins (1920-1973)
Marjorie (Lineback) Fruhling (1922-1994)
Jim Lineback (1926-1987)
Lois (Lineback) Keller (1927-1994)

INTRODUCTION

Don Lineback was born on his Mom and Dad's ranch in the "Sandhills" of western Nebraska in 1932. He was the youngest of Paul and Ocia Linebacks' fourteen children.

Paul and Ocia Lineback were pioneering people who "homesteaded" in the Sandhills in 1911. In those harsh living conditions, with the severe winters, Paul and Ocia raised fourteen of their own children, plus finished raising seven of Paul's brothers and sisters, due to the sudden death of Grandmother Lineback. In addition, Paul and Ocia raised four grandchildren during their pre-teen years. This all took place over a forty year period of time.

Don wrote this story with the help of his five remaining brothers and sisters. Don and his wife, Norma, who live in New York, raised five children of their own. Because of inquiries and interest of his grandchildren, Don feels this story should be told so that everyone, especially the second and third generations of Paul and Ocia Lineback, will never forget their origins.

Don Lineback
204 Church Avenue
Ballston Spa, NY 12020

My sister, Lois (1938), who made a major contribution in research of this book.

FOREWORD

As the years pass, we see one example after another of someone who offers what he has, and it becomes just what is needed by other persons or a situation. Such times call to mind the Bible story of the boy with his lunch of barley loaves and fish, who was in the great crowd listening to Jesus. The boy's loaves and fish, when blessed by Jesus, fed the thousands gathered on the hillside to hear His words.

In Nebraska's Sandhills, springtime of 1913, an epidemic of scarlet fever followed thaws of the worst blizzard many residents could remember. Young Paul and Ocia Lineback and their neighbors kept their children isolated as much as possible on their homesteads; even passing neighbors or peddlers were dealt with outside if that could be managed.

In June, a telegram notified the young couple that Paul's mother had died unexpectedly, and they had to make the train trip to Grand Island to handle funeral arrangements and look after Paul's seven younger brothers and sisters, now orphaned.

In the train coach, they made beds on the seats nearest the rest room for their one-year-old Helen and frail two-months-old Homer. As the train's wheels clicked their way east through the rolling hills and into farming country, they repeatedly reviewed the situation, though it remained the same: The seven orphaned siblings should grow up together if possible. Paul and Ocia had only their three-room sod house to offer, but they believed they could add two frame rooms to it. A decision had to be reached, and in their faith at ages 23 and 20 respectively, they reached it.

A sod schoolhouse was built that summer and on some Sundays families gathered there for Sunday School. They had no minister, but sang hymns and discussed religion. They brought food for the noon meal, and the children played while adults enjoyed the afternoon visiting.

Paul and Ocia's "loaves and fish" had been offered lovingly and in trust of the Lord. In the form of meat and potatoes, coleslaw and biscuits, clean clothes and beds, loving guidance in work habits, fairness, and trust in God, their "loaves and fish" shaped the lives of their foster children as well as those of the fourteen children born to them.

A generation later, monthly meetings of Sunday School were being held at various ranches, each participating family taking a turn. The Reverend Ernest G. Larsen, living between Bingham and Ellsworth, was usually present to lead devotions with one of his brief, unforgettable sermons.

I remember many precepts voiced by that wise, truly Christian man, the abundance of food brought by ranch families, the visiting, and the afternoon races.

The Linebacks' daughter Helen and I had reached the dignities of marriage and young motherhood, but we sometimes yielded to a coaxing summer wind and raced with the youngsters, despite the high heeled pumps that all young women wore on Sundays of those years. My racing was suspended for a while after the day I ran down into a gopher hole, did a ground loop, and came up with a sprained ankle.

Most of all, I remember the affection shown Mr. and Mrs. Lineback by their children and foster children, and the mother's beautiful soprano voice, leading the singing. It was said that her favorite hymn was *"The Old Rugged Cross"* and that she sang it often when working in her home. At those ranch meetings, she led us in singing it and other loved, familiar hymns, including the youngsters' favorite for its lively cadence, assuring us that *"There'll Be No Dark Valley When Jesus Comes."*

We sat to listen to a lesson or sermon; stood to pray or sing, and her face was glowing with the joy of being there, the trust in God's constant presence, as she sang His praises in that lovely voice, knowing so well the words and music that a child or two close beside her could feel the patting of her hand or its caring touch on a shoulder

Author Lineback has pictured well the joys and emergencies of ranch life in the rolling sandhills, and the little traditions that grow within a family. He knew that on his fifth birthday there would be a cake, and among his gifts would be a sturdy little milkstool made by his father, so now he could milk with the big boys.

There were graduations, weddings, and new little grandchildren in the passing years; then four little grandsons came to share the love and security of the Lineback home. Two were in lower grades of school; one was old enough to save steps for his busy grandmother, and one was a toddler. As they finished supper, the author recalls, Paul Lineback would lift the little fellow from his highchair to settle on his lap, letting him play with the well-anchored pocket watch while its owner read the paper.

During Memorial Day weekend two years ago, members of our Pollard family wandered a little after we had visited our loved ones' graves in the Alliance Cemetery. A brother and his wife, Dick and Ellen, paused with me beside the graves where Mr. and Mrs. Lineback rest among old friends and neighbors in that lovely setting.

"'God has no hands but ours,'" Dick quoted softly in tribute to that devoted couple. We knew that to guide twenty-five trusting youngsters into cheerful, productive lives. He had needed only theirs.

Ruth VanAckeren
Omaha, Nebraska
April 2, 1996

Ruth VanAckeren has written three books on Sandhills subjects, the most recent co-authored with Robert M. Howard, titled *Lawrence Bixby, Preserver of the Old Spade Ranch.*

December 8, 1994

Dear Maria,

Your mother told us that you have a project in school to have grandparents write about how things were different when they were young compared to now, when you are young. I would love to reminisce with you about how things were different. It is a very long period of time and you must realize that things do change.

As you know, I came from a very large family of fourteen children. We lived on a ranch in Nebraska. All of us kids had to work, doing our chores morning and night, like milking the cows, and feeding the pigs and chickens. During the school year, we walked about three fourths of a mile, out through the pasture to school.

Since it is now that time of the year, I want to tell you about what our Christmas was like. Christmas was always a special time for us. Because there were so many children, we knew that we would only get one gift each. We always had lots of food so we went about making it the best Christmas we could. The one I remember most was when I was about ten years old.

Your great grandfather decided that particular year he would raise turkeys for a local creamery. He had to get them in the spring when they were small, feed them through the summer and sell them back to the creamery just before Thanksgiving. Besides grain, turkeys love to eat grasshoppers and there was lots of grasshoppers out through the hay meadows. It was Dad's plan to have us kids herd the turkeys out through the fields daily so they could eat the grasshoppers. He told us that when we had done that, he would give us each

$5.00 to spend on Christmas. So sure enough, when he sold the turkeys we got the $5.00 and on a Saturday, just before Christmas, our parents took us shopping.

What a Christmas that was. I had asked my mother for ice skates that Christmas. I knew how to skate with hand-me-down skates from my older brothers and sisters, but I had never had my very own skates. There was this large lake just a short distance from our house and it was great for skating in the winter. My mother said that she would see. That usually meant that if she could find them, she would get them. I was in the "clouds." We had a Christmas play at school the day before Christmas. My brothers and sisters and I decided we would invite our neighbor friends over for an ice skating party on Christmas night.

We got up Christmas morning and did our chores, ate breakfast and then we got to open our presents. I got my skates! We headed for the lake and we skated in the morning, came in and ate dinner and went back skating in the afternoon. We came in and did our chores, ate supper and started making plans for our skating party. We asked Dad if we could build a fire near the ice for our party. He said yes and even helped to get it started. Our neighbors came and we had a great time skating and getting warm by the fire. Unbeknown to me at the time, our sisters had used part of their money to buy marshmallows, so we even had those to roast over the fire. Mom even let us stay out until about midnight and we really had a great time.

Things are really good now, Maria, but I will always have those memories to think about. I often do and you should always remember your childhood. I'm sure you will and it is nice. I love you.

-Grandpa

CONTENTS

FOURTEEN PLUS

1. THE HOMESTEADERS

From the time of the American Revolution, the disposition of the western frontier lands of the United States had been the subject of great concern to Congress. By 1862, most of the good lands east of the Mississippi River had passed into private hands. The eastern population was expanding and the idea was spreading that the federally owned lands of the West should be used to encourage western migration and settlement. It was on May 20, 1862 that Congress passed the Homestead Act, which was signed into law by President Lincoln.

Land west of the 100th meridian was known as the "Great American Desert;" at that time, few believed it was feasible to apply the Homestead Act to it. Under the act, a settler could file for ownership on 160 acres of land with the stipulation that he would live on it for five years and put $800 worth of improvements on it. At the end of that time, the land would be deeded to the settler.

The railroads were pressing west and the need for settlement was becoming more and more necessary for economic reasons. An advertisement was placed in the eastern press by the railroad, telling of the lands open for homesteading in the west. There was very little money and the thought of living off the land became very appealing. Floods of settlers soon started arriving.

William Alford Lineback was born on August 31, 1865 in Peoria, Illinois. He was to become my grandfather. That was the year that General Lee surrendered to General Grant during the Civil War. It was also the year President Lincoln was assassinated.

Milly Hardy was born on September 18, 1869 in Port Clinton, Ohio. She was to become my grandmother. I don't know how these two met, but I am sure that it was due to the migration of the people from the east. They both settled in Nebraska. According to the records on the birth of their children, they lived in several towns around the eastern part of Nebraska and one child was born in Fort Dodge, Iowa. They finally settled on a small farm in Gibbon, Nebraska.

Paul Silas Lineback was born August 28, 1890 in Grant, Nebraska. He was the second oldest of eleven children born to Grandmother and Grandfather Lineback. He was to become my dad.

Ocia Belle Dwiggins was born March 7, 1893 in Madison County, Indiana. She was the second youngest of eleven children of Grandmother and Grandfather Dwiggins. Her family migrated to Gibbon, Nebraska in the early 1900's. They later returned to Indiana. She was to become my mother.

***

In the 1880's and 1890's, many things were happening for the settlers. They soon homesteaded on the farm lands of eastern Nebraska that ran along the rivers of the state. Because this was tillable farm land, the Homestead Act that provided 160 acres worked very well for those homesteaders and they prospered.

There was, however, another large area of the state that was quite different. It was some 15,000 to 20,000 square miles of sandy hills that were covered with long grass. Because of the sandy soil, hilly terrain and the constant wind, it was not suitable for farming. The 160-acre tracts provided in the Homestead Act wouldn't work here.

This vast area became known as the "Sandhills." The Nebraska State Historical Society commemorates the "discovery" of the Sandhills that, in part, reads as follows:

"The Sandhills, Nebraska's most unique physiographic feature, covers about one-fourth of the state. The sandy soil acts like a giant sponge, soaking up rain and forming a vast underground reservoir. Hundreds of permanent lakes are found here. However, the same sandy soil makes the area unsuitable for cultivation. Grasses flourish, making the Sandhills ideal cattle country. Although the Sandhills were long considered 'an irreclaimable desert', cattlemen had begun to discover the Sandhills potential as range land by the early 1870's."

In the 1870's, the Spade Cattle Company came into existence. It was owned by Bartlett Richards. He bought out several small homesteaders who filed and "proved up" on 160 acre homesteads of lush meadow lands near the Niobrara River that runs through northern Nebraska. Richards' vision was to form a headquarters on these homesteads and have free government grazing land to raise cattle. It worked and all the "cattle barons" in the state were very prosperous and powerful. They attempted to shut out the small homesteaders by getting a federal leasing law passed that would assure them land for their cattle empires. They almost succeeded.

This was at a time when the U.S. Government was trying to settle the west, at the same time Jesse James and his brother, Frank, organized a band of outlaws. Their family had supported the confederacy during the Civil War. They ran rampant through the neighboring states of Missouri and Kansas, robbing small town banks and trains, until Jesse's death in 1882. He was shot in the back of the head by one of his own gang members for a $10,000 reward offered by the governor of Missouri.

The state started thinking about settling the area with more than a few large empires. It was soon evident that the 160-acre homesteads established by the Homestead Act could not apply to the Sandhills of Nebraska. More land was needed to carve out a living. Nebraska Senator Moses P. Kincaid proposed a revision to the Homestead Act In 1904, enabling a settler to receive a 640-acre tract of land under the same provisions as the original Homestead Act. It was passed and signed into law by President Theodore Roosevelt.

GRANDFATHER LINEBACK

In the mid 1900's, Grandmother and Grandfather Lineback were buying a farm in Gibbon, Nebraska. In those days they paid the mortgage once a year. In 1909 it was getting close to the time to pay the mortgage; however, they did not have the money. Grandfather decided that he would leave the farm in the hands of his oldest son, Merle, and go to the silver mines in Wyoming and Colorado to work until he had enough money to pay the mortgage.

He obviously had worked the mines before because he had the tools of the trade with which to work. It is not known how long he was at the mines, but he notified Uncle Merle he was sending his tools home and that he would be following soon. His tools arrived, but he was never heard from again. Grandmother tried to find out what happened, but never did.

There was a lot of speculation as to what might have happened. Some thought because he had the money he'd made, he was robbed and killed at the mines. With the scant information I have been told, I believe that he may have gone to eastern South Dakota and started another family. However, that is far from being proven.

To say the least, this left Grandmother Lineback in a dire situation. She was alone and pregnant, with a large family to raise. She had the emotional support of Uncle Merle and Dad, but there was very little money and it was extremely difficult. She gave birth to twins, a boy and a girl, in December 1909. Uncle Kenneth progressed satisfactorily, but Bertha, the girl, being weak, died a month after birth. It was an exceptionally emotional time for my Dad to face the task of burying his little sister.

***

Learning of and reading the Kincaid Act, Mom's brother, Uncle Jack Dwiggins, decided he would go to Ellsworth, Nebraska and file on a homestead. Around 1910, he and his wife, Aunt Renee, and son, Lawrence, went to Ellsworth and got their homestead started. All state lands were divided into counties and further into townships and sections. Ellsworth is in Sheridan County; the county seat in Rushville, Nebraska.

We don't know what year Mom and Dad first met, but Aunt Hazel told my sister, Jean, that my Mom's family (Dwiggins) moved into a farm down the road from Grandfather and Grandmother Lineback's farm. They needed a broom and Grandfather Dwiggins sent my Mom there to borrow one. That is how Mom and Dad met.

Despite the hardship of helping his mother with the raising of this brothers and sisters, my Mom and Dad were married on

February 22, 1911. Dad began thinking of owning his own place where they could raise their family. He liked the idea of homesteading, but decided to wait so they could help his mother get settled. In the summer of 1911, they went to Ellsworth to see Uncle Jack's homestead. During that visit, Dad looked at the lands that were available for homesteads and after three trips to Rushville by horseback, he filed on their own piece of land.

They returned to Gibbon that summer and started the task of getting Grandmother Lineback settled. Mom was pregnant and gave birth to her first child January 23, 1912. That was my sister Helen, the first of a long line. Later in the spring of 1912, my Grandmother decided she would move to Grand Island, Nebraska. It was a railroad town that offered a greater chance of finding work so she could go on raising the seven children left at home. Mom and Dad helped her get settled.

It was now time for Mom, Dad and Helen to move west and get settled on their homestead. It was easier for them because Uncle Jack was there to meet them and they had a place to stay until they could get their homestead started.

There were several things to consider in selecting a homestead. Balance was needed, the balance of hay land to feed the cattle in the winter and grazing land for the summer. Their homestead was just such a place. There was water to consider: Where do you put the house and barns for shelter for the livestock and a plot for a garden? The hard work was just beginning. There were very severe winters to contend with; any kind of facilities were non-existent; the mode of travel was either on horseback or with a team of horses and a wagon, and mail from their families was very spotty and only came when someone could get to town to get it. Living off the land is a great dream, but it is a lot easier said than done. It was lonely, but they had each other and the start of their own family.

2. The Soddy

The first order of business was to build a sod house for their living quarters. Dad plowed the grassy ground near the site, about four to six inches deep and twelve to fifteen inches wide. That was about as shallow as you could go and have the grass roots to hold the soil together. The sod was laid in layers to form a wall. When the walls were all set, with openings for a door and windows, the roof was put on. It was made out of wood, as was the flooring.

The initial house was a long building divided into three rooms. The entrance brought you into the kitchen and combined dining room. A doorway further in would bring you into the living room and then to the doorway into Mom and Dad's bedroom. Each room had windows that were set to the outside of the ledge making a deep window ledge. With that done and secured, the structure became Mom and Dad's initial sod house, thereafter known as the "Soddy."

The next order of business was water. In the sandhills, there was no shortage of water underground. Wells had to be drilled to bring it to the surface. It was a lot of work but a simple mechanical operation. I don't know how Dad first started, but in later years he use to "witch" for water. He would cut a fork from a tree branch, preferably an apple tree branch, a simple Y. You would hold the fork by the two ends with the single end straight out in front of you and start walking. When you ran into a water vein underneath the ground, the end would twist down towards the ground.

In drilling for a well, they would dig down as far as they could with a shovel then they would start a length of two inch pipe down in the hole. With the use of a three-quarter-inch pipe inside the two-inch pipe and lake water, they could "chug" the sand out of the two inch pipe and work it down into the ground. To find good running and drinking water, Dad would go down anywhere from 15 to possibly 60 feet. After finding good water, they would insert an one and one-half-inch pipe with a sand screen on the bottom, into the two-inch pipe. They would put a hand pump on it and pump the water to the surface. Later when they had cattle, they would build windmills that had a fan, gear box and pump and the wind would turn the fan and pump the water to the surface. It would pump the water into what we always called a "horse tank" for the livestock to drink from. The water for the house was pumped from the hand pump and carried into the house.

The exact date that Mom and Dad moved into their soddy is not known. It is also hard to say what work may have been done next at the homestead. There certainly was a lot to be done. There were outbuildings to be built for the cattle, pigs and chickens. They needed a plot for a garden and fences around the homestead property to contain the animals, they had to build "outhouse" for a bathroom. That became known as the "privy" and it stayed with the family as long as they lived in the sandhills.

There was cattle, pigs and chickens to be bought. Money was scarce, but Dad bought what he could and built his herds up as well as he could. It very quickly became a way of life for ranchers to borrow from neighbors. They frequently exchanged things like equipment and horses to work with. A bond developed among homesteaders that went on to become life-long friendships; they were all in this together and needed each other for survival.

In the fall of 1912, Mom became pregnant again. She had Helen to care for and winter was coming. It turned out to be a very severe winter with a hard blizzard that came in March 1913. At that time, the Spade Cattle Company was grazing cattle on the school sections around Tin Can Lake. This was an area two miles due west of the homestead which Dad later leased. Due to the winds, the Spade cattle started drifting with the wind and onto the lake, where forty of them drowned. Dad and Uncle Jack got the job of pulling them out of the lake with a team of horses, skinning them and selling the hides.

My brother, Homer, was born on May 3, 1913. He was very small, weighing only three and a half pounds. This presented some problems. He was delivered by Mrs. Louden, a neighbor lady who was a midwife. Midwives in those times had no training, they were simply women who helped other women have their babies because there were no doctors available. Grandmother Lineback also came up from Grand Island to help. Seeing the situation with Homer, they fashioned an "incubator" out of a cardboard box and made a cotton lining for it. It worked just fine because Homer grew to adulthood. When things settled down and Mom regained her strength, Grandmother returned to Grand Island and to her family.

It was a great shock when Mom and Dad received a telegram telling them that Grandmother Lineback had died unexpectedly on June 30, 1913. They left by train as soon as they could to take care of her burial. Another gigantic task faced them when they arrived. What would they do with the remaining seven brothers and sisters? Grandmother's brother, Uncle Ward Hardy and his wife, Aunt Grace, said that they would take the three youngest to live with them. Dad, being very family oriented said no, that he and Mom would take all of them to the homestead. Mom, who was only twenty years old, with two of her own children, found it to be a very giant step. Because of their ages, there was an immediate need for a school. It was decided that Aunt Anna, nearly 18, would stay with Uncle Ward along with the three youngest, while Dad could make arrangements at the homestead. With that done, Mom and Dad and the three oldest, Aunt Edith, Uncle Cecil and Aunt Marie, returned to their soddy home in the Sandhills.

EXTENDED FAMILY

That summer there was a major project carried out at the homestead. Dad built a sod school house on the property. It was built there because at that time there were no other children old enough, in that area, to go to school. The big concern was to provide schooling for Dad's brothers and sisters. A teacher was hired and they were to start school in the fall.

That schoolhouse also became a social center for the sandhills area. They started having Sunday School services there. Although there was no minister, the neighbors would gather to sing hymns and discuss religion. They brought food to share and visited with each other. At other times, they would have social functions where the women would fix box lunches, wrap them with no names on them and the men would bid on them. The proceeds going to the school. Even the young girls and boys participated.

Somehow Dad acquired a victrola record machine and records and dances would be held. Dad loved to dance and was quite good at it. Aunt Marie told my sister, Jean, that when Dad got the extended family together he told them, "you all have to work and each will have chores to do but we will also have fun dancing on Saturday nights." Everyone did what they were told and Dad taught all his brothers and sisters how to dance a lot of different dances like schottisches and waltzes.

During the summer of 1913 two new wooden frame rooms were added to the soddy. With that improvement done, Aunt Anna brought the three remaining siblings, Aunts Hazel and Ruth and Uncle Kenneth, to the homestead to live. They were together again and with all that had happened to them, it must have been a very hectic year. It was time to get on with life and there was much more to be done.

Providing for the Family

It became very obvious from the beginning how Dad intended to homestead his land. He started by buying a few milk cows. These would provide milk to drink; the excess was separated and the cream was shipped to an eastern market by train from Ellsworth. The skim milk was fed to the small calves weaned from their mothers so they could be milked. With the rest of the skim milk as a base, Dad would make a mash of grains and milk, called "slop," to feed to the pigs. The calves, when old enough, would be put out to pasture until they were big enough to butcher. The females of both cattle and pigs were kept for breeding purposes. That is how Dad built his herds up. Late every fall, just before the frost hit, Dad would butcher a pig and a steer. Left in an unheated building, the meat would freeze and keep through the winter. This provided the family with all the beef and pork that they needed to eat.

Mom was also instrumental in raising chickens. They had gotten a few chickens and as they laid eggs, Mom would gather them, pick out the most uniform ones, and save them for hatching baby chickens. You could always tell when old hens were ready to "set." They placed the old hen in a separate coop, with twelve or thirteen eggs marked with the date, and in three weeks little chicks would hatch. They were cute little things but they weren't hatched to be cute. As they grew they became an excellent source of chicken meat.

Milk provided other things also. Mom would churn the cream to make butter; she also made cottage cheese from sour milk. Cream would be kept in a cold water tank. About once or twice a week, it would be taken to Ellsworth by team and wagon and shipped by railroad to an eastern market. They would pay for the cream by check. Whomever made that trip would get the mail and then go to the store to get whatever staples were needed. The railroad also provided a means to ship cattle and pigs to an eastern market for slaughtering.

Dad was excellent with gardens. He raised everything from seed. Because of the short growing season, some plants had to be started before the frost stopped. Dad fashioned a "hot bed." He dug a bed down about three feet, put in a thick layer of cow manure and topped it off with dirt. He planted the seeds in late March or early April. The top was covered with glass storm windows. This provided sunlight to the plants during the daytime and yet protected them from the frost.He always planted the full garden around May 10 because, according to him, that was when the danger of frost had passed. Other vegetables were planted from seed and the "hot bed" plants such as tomatoes, cabbage and peppers were well underway by May so they were transplanted in the garden.

During the later part of summer and early fall, Mom and the girls would start canning. It was a grueling job. They had to use the stove and as with all cooking, it was hard work. There were no trees and firewood for fuel was non-existent. The cattle dung from the pastures would dry and that became the source of fuel. They became known as "cow chips." Cow chips would burn extremely fast and very hot for a short period of time. It was often said that cow chips burned either too hot or too cold. To say the least, it was extremely difficult to cook with them. Dad and the boys would gather the chips by team and wagon and pile them in the chip house or sometimes they would overflow into the yard. Sometimes the pile of cow chips would be bigger than the house.

It was up to Mom and the girls to bring in the chips and start the fire burning. Just bringing in the chips and taking out the ashes were big jobs. Chips were used for all the cooking and with canning it was just an additional burden. In the fall, Dad would get a wagon load of coal from the Ellsworth store to supplement the cow chips. The coal provided a more even burning fire which was especially necessary for heating the house in the winter time. They could not afford it all the time.

Mom canned everything from vegetables to meats and even fruits when they could get them from the Ellsworth store. Just what year it started I don't know, but there was a Sandoz orchard north of the homestead. Mom and Dad bought fruits from them, like apples, crabapples, cherries, plums and so forth. All canned foods were placed in a "root cellar" that Dad built. It was cave-like, dug partially underground with a wood and dirt covering. A bin was built for potatoes and other root vegetables. Carrots and turnips buried in sand in the root cellar would keep all winter. Shelving was made for storing all the canned goods in glass jars. Root cellars also became places of protection from cyclones; upright buildings wouldn't protect you from the extremely high winds.

Mom and Dad also used mail order catalogs for needed items. There were cooking utensils, canning jars and material and thread for family clothing. Mom was an excellent seamstress who made most of the family clothing. My sister, Lois, wrote that Mom could make almost anything. If she didn't have a pattern, she would measure them up with a newspaper and cut a pattern herself. Anyway, the job got done.

There wasn't much need to buy most foods because they grew the majority of them. At that time, the items they had to buy were either ordered or bought at the Ellsworth store. They were items like flour, sugar, coffee, salt, baking powder, baking soda, yeast for bread and lye for soap. Mom made lye soap out of rendered pig fat and lye. It was strong and they used it for washing clothes and anything that needed cleaning. I remember using it for bathing but you had to be careful not to leave it on the skin very long or it would burn.

3. LIFE ON THE HOMESTEAD

My brother, Vern, was born on December 21, 1914. World War I was raging in Europe. It seemed the whole country was in a turmoil. Mom's brother, Uncle Hi, had been drafted and was serving in Germany. It was a scary time. Defense plants were being built and opening in Lakeside and Antioch, Nebraska. They produced potash, which is made of alkali, for the war effort. Those towns became "boom" towns and created many jobs for men. They were about fifteen to twenty miles from the homestead. Aunt Anna met and married Art Shigley, who worked at the potash plants. They moved to Alliance, Nebraska and raised four children during their lives.

About that time, Dad decided that the sod chicken house was too small for the growing number of chickens they had, and decided to build a wood frame building for the chickens. He tore off the roof of the old building, leaving the sod walls standing. It was a great place for the kids to play. Homer, who was about two, got carried away and fell off one of the walls and broke his arm. There was a doctor in Bingham, Nebraska some eight to ten miles away, so Mom and Dad made a bed in the wagon and drove there by team to get his arm set.

Doctors were very scarce in those days. With the sparse settlement of homesteaders and the few small towns, there was one in Bingham and then, as the potash plants began to boom, there was a "company doctor" in Antioch who would see other people on an emergency basis. His name was Doctor Moore. Babies were most always delivered by midwives and family care always came from a meager supply of over-the-counter medical supplies and a lot of common sense.

My sister, Margaret, was born on February 3, 1916. Mrs. Adams, a neighbor, came as a midwife and helped with her delivery. The Adams' were in the Sandhills for a short time, until tragedy hit their family. They had two sons who were playing in a sand bank and dug a cave into the bank. It caved in, killing them both. They left the Sandhills shortly after that.

Mom's brother, Uncle Dave and Aunt Iva, came from Gibbon and homesteaded on a 160-acre tract of land west and south of the homestead until around 1923. It was great for Mom to have more of her family around. They proved up on their property, and Dad bought it when they returned to Gibbon to live.

My brother, Paul Jr., was born on October 19, 1917. I'm not sure which midwife assisted with that birth, but it could very well have been Aunt Iva. As Paul Jr. grew up, he acquired a nickname and to my knowledge he very rarely was called Paul. It was said that when he was small, his rear end would waddle like a duck when he walked. He was dubbed "Duck" and it stuck with him throughout his life.

In the spring of 1918, Uncle Jack had proved up on their homestead and decided they would sell out and move back to the eastern part of the state. He sold his homestead to another homesteader named Fred Trinkle. Mr. Trinkle later leased the land to Jim and Min Johnston, who became Mom and Dad's lifelong friends. The Trinkle's eventually sold Uncle Jack's homestead to Lou Munger. They also became lifelong friends of my parents. The Johnston's moved to a place they bought west of Lakeside and lived there the rest of their lives. All the kids went to school in the little sod school house on Mom and Dad's homestead. The Sandhills was certainly filling up with settlers.

ACQUIRING LAND

Some of the homesteaders were not so fortunate in homesteading. Several of them couldn't stand the harshness of the living conditions or didn't have the balanced land to make homesteading work and move out to other places. Maybe it was the combination of the two, because it was a hard life. Most of those people would stay on their homesteads and scratch out a living until they completed the five-year residency requirement and then sold out.

Dad bought two such homesteads around that time. They

Homer with Polo, our first pony.

were always called the Reiger and Bishop sections. That gave him 1,920 acres of land that he owned, and provided him with a lot of grazing land to expand his herd. These sections were mostly grazing land and didn't provide the necessary hay land he needed. Doc Coe, another homesteader just north of the homestead, wanted to lease his parcel of land. It had some grazing land but, more importantly, it also had some much needed hay land. Dad leased it for several years until he could get hay land to balance his ranch.

Aunt Edith went to work at the Spade Ranch as a cook for the hired help. There she met and married Charlie Crofutt. They set up housekeeping on the Spade property, eventually settling in Wyoming and raising nine children. Aunt Marie went to visit them at the Spade, where she met and married Joe Steggs. He was the postmaster for the Spade and also ran a small store on the ranch. They eventually settled in Denver, Colorado and raised eight children.

Much to everyone's relief, Uncle Hi came home from the war in 1918. He came and stayed with Mom and Dad for awhile, working for Dad and some of the other homesteaders. He also worked at the potash plants and lived in both Lakeside and Antioch. He met and married Fern Whitcome, a school teacher. They lived on a small homestead just south of Mom and Dad for a short time, then moved to Scottsbluff and made their home there.

In the fall of 1918, it was decided the little sod school house was too small for all the kids in the area and a more permanent one was needed. There was a wood frame building on the Adams' homestead that wasn't being used. The neighbors got together, formed a school district, bought the school building and moved it to a central location on one of the school sections. It was about three-quarters of a mile from our homestead.

Dad always said that when he was a boy he wanted a pony and, if he could, all his kids would have a pony. Around the time when my older brothers and sister were eight to ten years old, he bought one. It was named "Polo." Polo was with the family for several years. From that time on we always had a pony on the ranch, and even after Mom and Dad went into semi-retirement, there was always a pony for the grandchildren.

My brother, Rodney, was born on April 20, 1919. That summer Dad decided they needed a big barn to house the cattle in the lower part and to store hay in an overhead loft to protect it in the winter months. With the help of Jake Zieg, a neighbor friend, and the boys, Dad built the barn. The growing herd of milk cows would be milked in the lower half and the cows that were having calves could be brought in and sheltered. Horses were also kept in the barn. As hay was cut in the summer, it would be brought in and stored in the loft for winter feed. The barn was a great improvement for the Homestead.

My sister, Catherine, was born on November 7, 1920. That next spring, in 1921, Dad bought a two-room wood frame house from the Adams' homestead, moved it to the homestead and added it to the soddy. It also was a great improvement for the living conditions for the family.

Margaret's Story

My sister, Margaret, writes about how the household chores were done, things she remembers from when she about five years old.

"Every one of the girls shared in cooking three meals a day. Mom was, of course, the leader and planned each meal. Breakfast was pancakes and whatever else we might have, like bacon, ham and, if the chickens were laying, eggs. We also had oatmeal every day. That was a lot of food, but everyone had been up for a long time and had done the outside chores like milking the cows, feeding the chickens and the pigs. The kids always drank milk and Mom and Dad had coffee. Lunch or dinner, as it was called, was easy. Someone (we took turns) would pack a sandwich of homemade bread and butter for each of the kids going to school. Occasionally, if available, we also got a piece of fruit and sometimes cake or cookies. About 3 p.m., Mom would ask: "What shall we have for supper?" Generally no one knew, so she'd say, "I'll think on it." About 4:30, she'd have it figured out. The school kids would be coming home and she would get them started on the evening chores.

"Dinner, or supper as it was called, was a real team effort for the girls. The little ones would set the table and the rest helped Mom with whatever had to be done. We had great fresh vegetables from the garden in the summer and home canned ones in the winter months. In the summer months we had lots of fried chicken; during the hunting season Dad and the boys took a rifle to the field and shot grouse, wild ducks or rabbits, and that really tasted good. If nothing else was available we always had canned meats. In the winter we always had fresh beef and pork. It seemed that we always had plenty of meat of one kind or another.

"We grew most everything we ate. No wonder we had so many chores to do. I remember the sweet corn patch. Duck, Rodney and I became known as the "weed pullers" and had to pull the weeds out of that corn patch. By the time we got the thistles, tumbleweeds and sun flowers (they hurt my hands so bad and leaked that sticky resin all over) and pig weeds, which we kept apart from the rest to feed to the pigs, all pulled out, Dad would come strolling by to say "howdy." He would then suggest that he could still see weeds in the first part we had pulled, and he'd tell us to start over. I have to admit he was nearly always right.

"That wasn't the last of the corn patch either. After the corn was all picked and canned or dried and stored away for the winter, we had to cut the stalks down for feed for the pigs.

"By now it was fall with the winter fast approaching. We had to get ready for school. Mom and the older girls were busy sewing everyone new school clothes. The boys had "store bought" overalls and socks, but as far as I remember the rest of our school clothes were sewn by Mom, Helen, Ruth and Hazel. Of course we

The homestead taken after the barn was built (circa 1922).

each had a pair of shoes to start the school year. They may have been hand-me-downs. I sure remember coats, overshoes, caps and scarves being handed down.

"We always had to go to school, walking over the hills to get there. On stormy days, Dad always said "stay together." I was small and could never seem to keep up. Homer and Kenneth took turns carrying me on their backs. On the weekends, and sometimes after school, we would pick up cow chips to keep the cooking stove going. We kept the shed full until the snow got so deep it covered the chips. The older boys and Dad had other things to do, like taking care of the cattle, so the cow chip picking was done by the "weed pullers," Rodney, Duck and me. Sometimes Mom and the big girls helped us; however, they were usually busy with canning, sewing or taking care of the little ones and the babies. There was always plenty for everyone to do.

"In the fall of the year, Dad and the boys would butcher one steer and one or two pigs. They would be hung in an outbuilding where they would freeze and keep all winter long. They would make up hams, to be cured, and bacon and grind up sausage. Using small intestines, that had been turned inside out and cleaned very thoroughly, the sausage would be stuffed. The hams were smoked as was the bacon, to cure for use during the winter. Meats for the summertime had to be canned and stored in the root cellar.

"Mom also made lye soap from the pig fat. When butchering, the pig fat was cut off and tossed in a big tub. She took and cut it into two inch squares and cooked it, rendering it into grease. She would then add a mixture of lye and water and kept cooking. It had to be constantly stirred to keep from scorching. They would then strain it into a shallow pan to sit and cool. After cooling, it was solid and was cut into squares; then it was soap. It was mainly used for washing clothes, but it also was used for washing dishes, floors and baths.

"We were a pretty self-sustaining family. Very few items of groceries had to be purchased from the store. Some needed items were ordered from a sales catalog and Mom also bought from vendors. Mom and Dad would go to Ellsworth in the fall of the year and buy the winter supply of flour (twelve to fourteen bags, one or two 100-pound bags of sugar, yeast and baking powder for bread, baking soda, cocoa and coffee). Other items were either purchased by ordering from Sears and Roebuck or through vendors. Such items as spices, sewing supplies (like needles, thread and pins). She also got yardage to make girls dresses and the boys shirts. All of Dad's overalls, as well as the boys, and all the shoes were gotten from Sears and Roebuck."

PEDDLERS

Peddlers started coming through the country. They traveled by teams of horses and sold a variety of wares. One was an old Assyrian man who peddled material and household items. He traveled by a four-horse team and had a driver with him to handle the horses. He spoke very broken English, was a rough old guy and didn't have many manners, but he always left everyone laughing. His name was "Old George the Peddler" and his driver was Joe. My sister, Margaret, tells of him coming to the homestead one time when Mom and Dad weren't home. As usual he asked to spend the night. Aunt Hazel was in charge and she told him no because Mom and Dad had gone to Ellsworth to meet Aunt Marie and Uncle Joe who were coming on the train to visit with all their children. That wasn't really so, but George believed her, so as he climbed back upon his "Wag" (as he called it) he said, "Damn, when I die and go to hell I'll be put out by 'Ball' Lineback's relations." That became a standing joke from then on. Another of the peddlers was from the Larkin Company.

That was a membership club that sold household furniture. The club was formed and the women would meet once a month at someone's house to look over and purchase furniture for their homes. Through this club, the women decided that they should have a monthly Sunday School. They picked the first Sunday of the month and alternated homes for the service. There was no minister available, but they would gather and sing hymns and have a bible study for the kids. It was an all-day affair with a pot luck dinner at noon time. Sunday School stayed in the Sandhills for many years.

QUARANTINE

Communicable diseases were always a threat to the homesteaders. Due to the lack of doctors, everyone prayed that nothing serious would ever happen. Measles and chicken pox passed through the school with little effect other than being sick for a few days. In the fall of 1920, a neighbor, Warren Wilcox, who had gone away to high school, brought the small pox home to his family. It was in turn brought to the little sod schoolhouse. It became a severe epidemic. Aunt Hazel and Helen caught it first. They had fairly mild cases. Dad was next and he was much sicker. Uncle Cecil was working at another homestead and he was notified to come home to help with the chores and ranch work.

Mom was next and being so close to the others that were sick, she had a very severe case. Doctor Moore was sent for because she was so very, very sick. Before coming to the homestead, Doctor Moore notified the county at Rushville and then came right out to the homestead. The first thing that the doctor did was vaccinate all those that hadn't gotten it yet. Then he started nursing Mom back to health. The state quarantined the homestead with a big red "Quarantined" sign.

My sister, Margaret, writes that "I was only four (almost five) that very cold and blizzardy January of 1921, when Mom came down with the small pox. Catherine was only three or four months old and Duck, Rodney and I were quarantined which meant we had to stay in the house with Mom and Dad. Dad rode on horseback to Antioch to get the company doctor to come. I don't remember who took care of Mom but I think it may have been one of the neighbor ladies. Most of this I remember being talked about, but I do remember trying to help take care of Mom as well as taking care of Catherine. I would rock her in my little rocking chair. She cried a lot because she had chicken pox and she also had to learn to take the bottle. Vern, Duck, Rodney and I all had light cases of small pox, so we were immune by then. Dr. Moore vaccinated all the rest, Hazel, Ruth, Kenneth, Helen and Homer. They all went to stay with Aunt Iva and Uncle Dave on their homestead. They came home on weekends to clean the house, cook food and bake bread for the coming week. We were sure glad to see them and we all visited Mom through her bedroom window."

When Mom started to show improvement, Dr. Moore told Aunt Hazel to butcher a chicken and they made chicken broth. It must have worked, because Mom started to gain her strength back. Uncle Dave and Aunt Iva were allowed through the quarantine and they came to help. They were given shots and their help was very much needed.

During the sickness, the chores were left up to Uncle Cecil, Uncle Kenneth, Homer and Vern. One day while going to the barn to milk the cows, Homer bet them all he could walk all the way to the barn backwards. They took him up on it and opened the gates for him. He backed into an open icy horse tank and got soaking wet. Dr. Moore, who was there, told Homer to take a hot bath and sit by the stove. He never did get sick. As Mom got stronger, Dr. Moore left to return to his practice in Antioch. Although everyone helped out, it was still a very scary time for the family because Mom almost died. It took Mom and Dad a full year to recover.

During the time Aunt Iva and Uncle Dave lived on their homestead, they were a great help to Mom and Dad. During a sickness (such as the small pox epidemic), they were great moral support. They had two children, Dave Jr. and Bernice, while they lived on their homestead. Uncle Dave was great with kids.

HOLIDAYS

Mom always made sure we understood the meaning of and celebrated all of the holidays. Each one of us celebrated our birthdays with a birthday cake, usually with no candles, and most times with no presents, but it was a birthday and no one forgot. My sister, Margaret, also wrote, "We had very special Thanksgivings, very often shared with neighbors, Mom and Dad's special friends Jim and Min Johnston, and our relatives. We always had turkey and all the trimmings, homemade cranberry sauce and pumpkin and mincemeat pies. Christmas was a great time, both at school and at home. We started right after Thanksgiving planning and rehearsing the Christmas play at school. The teacher wrote the play, sometimes humorous and other times religious. We always sang lots of Christmas carols and the audience, mostly parents, would join in. We would draw names and exchange homemade gifts and then it was off to home to wait for our family Christmas.

"Our Christmas tree was usually a cutting off of a big cottonwood tree. Each branch would be wrapped in cotton and decorations would be what we made in school. There would be bright red and green colors and we would string long threads of popcorn and cranberries on the tree. We always got one gift each under the tree. It was like magic. On Christmas morning all the presents were there all wrapped in pretty paper and ribbons and tagged for each one. There were sleds and skates for the boys and dolls for the girls. We all had to share what few toys we got. Then it was dinner time and it was much like Thanksgiving plus the older girls had made homemade candy the night before and we usually had some hard candy that had been ordered from the catalogs. I can still see Dad sitting in the living room, amidst the wrapping paper and ribbons smoking his new pipe.

"We had nice Easters, too. We would gather all the eggs we had, hard boil and color them as best we could with crayons and watercolors. We would hide and look for them all day. When we found them, we would eat them. Some were saved for future school lunches. We were always told of the religious aspect of Easter."

My sister, Marjorie, was born on December 8, 1922. Mrs. Thompson was the midwife that helped with her delivery. Mrs. Thompson and her husband, Shorty, were neighboring homesteaders and friends of the family. She became the midwife that helped in delivering almost all the rest of us. Marjorie was a sickly baby due to a heart murmur. As soon as possible, she was taken to a doctor who told Mom and Dad that if she lived until three or four years of age, she more than likely would be fine.

In August 1924, Aunt Hazel met Bill Huber, a salesman who was working in and around that area. They were married and eventually settled in Alliance. They raised four children.

THE END OF THE SPADE EMPIRE

My sister, Jean, was born on May 1, 1924. Everything was beginning to change in the Sandhills. In the early 1900's, the Federal Government found the big cattle empires in total disregard of the Fencing Law as provided by the Kincaid Act. They had decided to ignore the law and continue grazing cattle in open territories. On November 12, 1906, a 40-count indictment was drawn up in Omaha, Nebraska, charging the cattlemen with fraud and conspiracy of the U.S. Government. The cattlemen paid people to file on section claims knowing that they would not live on it. In five years the lands would revert to the cattle empires and, therefore, they would maintain their huge empires. The owners of the Spade Ranch Empire, Bartlett Richards and Will Comstock, were convicted and sentenced to prison terms, thus ending the Spade Ranch Empire.

The Spade Ranch did live on. A man by the name of Lawrence Bixby, with the help of the Brass and Meyers Cattle Company, were able to legally purchase 25,000 acres (40 sections) that the empire had deeds for. There were three sections, 1,080 acres of school land that bordered Mom and Dad's homestead. This land was being used by the Spade Ranch. In the interest of getting rid of all undeeded land and complying with the law, Walter Wightman, the Ellsworth Postmaster and secretary-treasurer of the Spade Ranch, was able to obtain a twenty-five-year lease on these school properties for Mom and Dad. It gave them a very balanced ranch that could easily handle a sizable herd of cattle and the horses needed in order to work the land.

4. THE NEW HOUSE

*W*ith the leases in place for the school sections, Dad received permission to build a new house and outbuildings on one of the sections. There was a dire need since the old soddy was filled up with kids. The site that they selected for the house, barn, corrals and out buildings was perfect. It was snuggled right up against the rolling pasture hills, with the corrals emptying out into the pastures for the milk cows and the horses they needed for working the land. There was a good-sized hay meadow right in front of the house that provided four or five hay stacks and would probably feed the milk cows for most of the winter. There was a good-sized lake up close to the house. It was alkaline water and not fit to drink, but it was great for ice skating.

It would be a large project that would last for two years before it would be ready to move into. Dad laid out the plans for the house, barns and various outbuildings. He hired Jake Zieg, among others, and they got started. Of course my brothers were there to help, but they also had to take care of the haying and other ranching jobs.

Dad bought a large apartment building, from the potash plant in Lakeside. With World War I over, most of the potash plants were closed and the buildings left empty. They tore the building down and salvaged the lumber for the new house. They hauled the wood by a big wagon pulled by a four-horse team, to the ranch, making the trip every other day until they had all the material there. They worked on the house for the rest of 1924, all of 1925, and into the spring of 1926.

Compared to the old soddy, the new house was like a mansion. It was two stories, with a kitchen, dining room, living room, bathrooms and one bedroom on the first floor with five bedrooms upstairs. There was a pitcher pump in the kitchen so they

Jake Zieg (right) worked for Dad building the barn and ranch buildings on the homestead.

could draw water from inside the house and the bathroom had a sink for washing and a tub for bathing.

Of course there was still the trail out through the backyard to the outside privy with its old catalogs for toilet paper.

Sometime around the spring of 1926, a cyclone came through the homestead. No one was hurt because, I'm sure, they took shelter in the root cellar. The cyclone never touched the old soddy, but it damaged some of the outbuildings and completely blew down the barn. They salvaged what material they could and used it to build the barn at the new place.

My brother, Jim, was born on January 8, 1926. I am sure Mrs. Thompson assisted as the midwife. The new house was almost ready and plans were being made to move into it in the spring. There was still work to be done in securing the buildings and the horses, cows and chickens had to be moved and settled, but the time was getting close for the big move.

Moving Day

It was a great day that spring when the family loaded up the hay rack, with all the furniture and personal belongings and headed out to their new home, about one and a half miles away, on May 1, 1926 (which happened to be my sister Jean's birthday). It is said that they all walked, except baby Jim and Marjorie. She was still kind of sick and Dad told her it was her job to watch the baby. It was a great day for the family. Of course the haying and regular ranch work still had to be done.

Putting up hay for the livestock winter feed became a major summer project at the ranch, especially with the school sections

Moving Day, May 1, 1926. (L-R) Helen, holding baby Jim, Homer, Vern, Margaret, Duck, Rodney, Catherine, Marjorie and Jean, the nine who were born on the homestead.

that Mom and Dad had acquired. Haying seasons generally started just after the Fourth of July and would run through to the time that school started. It was usually completed by that time, but sometimes there was small jobs of bunching hay for additional feed and Dad would take care of that. First there was hay cutting, done with horse drawn mowers. These were mowers with a six to seven foot sickle bar. As the wheels turned, the sickle bar would move back and forth, cutting the hay. Next was the rake that would put the hay into win-rows. Then came the sweeping and stacking. The sweep, pulled by horses, would sweep the hay onto the stacker head. It would be pulled, by a team of horses, up over the top and onto the hay stack. The mowers and rake were machinery and had to be bought. The sweep, stacker and back stop were made of wood and built by Dad. It was quite an operation.

My sister, Lois, was born on August 27, 1927. She was the first to be born in the new house and the first, and only, one to be delivered by a doctor. Dr. Farmer came out to the ranch to deliver her. The living conditions were certainly improving for most of the Sandhills folks. Most had more livable houses and while there still wasn't much money, people could buy more.

BARN DANCES

The new barn that Dad had built on the ranch also became a big social attraction. It was said that the first dance held in the new barn was held before the roof was put on. It was an open air dance and it proved to be a lot of fun. The flooring in the hay loft wasn't very smooth but no one seemed to mind. In the late 1920's and early 1930's, barn dances were held two or three times during the summer. In the spring, when all the winter hay had been fed out and the loft was empty, the kids would sweep it clean.They would start making plans for the summer barn dances. The neighbors would be notified, benches would be rigged up around the walls, and all plans would be set. All the women would bring food for a pot luck evening snack and of course there was always coffee. They would dance to the music of Tom Roethler and John Louden on the fiddles and Shorty Thompson on the drums. The Hamilton family that lived a distance to the north sometimes came. They could play the guitars and they would join in. After their evening snack, a talent show of sorts would be put on and everyone would perform his or her particular talent. Mom could play the mouth harp and some of the men could jig. The babies and other small children would be put to bed in the house and others would be bedded down in the buggies and wagons. The dancing would go on until daybreak. Everyone learned to dance at a young age in those days. It was always a great party.

***

The Depression set in all over the United States in 1928. It was a severe situation that affected a lot of people. There wasn't any money for most people and with the lack of money and food, many were in desperate conditions. Mom and Dad, who had adapted to the art of living off the land, at least knew they would have food to eat. The problem was selling the cream, eggs and such that provided the money for the few necessities they needed. The price of cattle and pigs plummeted and that caused problems. However, the ranch was secure. They had their home and they just rolled with the times, as they always had.

During the Depression, President Franklin Roosevelt tried

to pull the country back up by establishing the Works Progress Administration. It became known as the WPA and it created projects around the country that provided jobs for men. One project was to build a road, out of alkaline mud, about a half mile from Ellsworth over the old Spade trail. The road, of course, didn't last because the rains would wash it away, but it did provide jobs. Uncle Floyd and Aunt Ruth stayed with the family for awhile during those times and Uncle Floyd worked for the WPA. He was paid one dollar a day.

Later Uncle Floyd built a small house on the old homestead land, about a quarter of a mile west of Mom and Dad's original homestead.They lived there for a short time before moving to the Jamison ranch, where Uncle Floyd began working. They lived there until approximately 1933, when the house burned down. That was during the same time Homer and Betty decided they were moving to Idaho.

5. Early Life on the Ranch

*W*ith the new house, barn and outbuildings, things certainly were improving. There were still hardships with getting the mail and, the severe winters never changed. We still walked to school, about the same distance, but from a different direction. The ranch was growing. Dad was starting to build up his herd of range cattle and the new barn he built had cow stanchions to hold about 40 milk cows. I don't ever remember us milking that many, but my brothers said they did milk that many at times.

First Car

Even though there were still harsh living conditions to contend with, life in the Sandhills was progressing. Transportation by team and wagon was slow and hard to say the least. The automobile had been invented and the old Spade wagon trail was there. It was just a two rut trail that ran through the countryside and ended in Ellsworth. Dad and his friend, Jim Johnston, decided they would each buy a car. They went by train to Denver, where each purchased an "Overland Touring Car," complete with isinglass windows. Neither had driven a car before, but somehow the salesman got them to the edge of Denver and they drove home. By the time they drove the 300 miles home, they knew how to drive their Overlands. The old Spade trail wasn't very suitable for cars, but they made it and having a car was a big improvement for the family.

The roads, running through the sandy soil, would often become clogged with deep sand dunes caused by the winds. It was treacherous going for cars. It was almost always necessary to carry a shovel for digging out when you got stuck. Usually in the spring of the year, all the neighbors would bed the roads run-

Cattle grazing on the summer Reiger range.

ning through their property with the remains of hay stack beds. This helped to prevent the sand from blowing and the cars could get through easier. It still was advisable to carry a shovel.

There were no driver licenses at the time. When they did come into existence, they were sold over-the-counter in grocery stores.

***

My sister, Phyllis, was born on January 11, 1929. Mrs. Thompson assisted as the midwife. The ranch was really beginning to shape up. Dad built a chicken house with a pen, and a milk house. The milk house had a water tank that was fed by a windmill. The separated cream was kept in the water tank where it could remain for longer periods of time before taking it to market. Around that time, the Alliance Creamery opened for business and the cream could be taken there to sell. There were stores opening up in Alliance that sold almost anything they needed and relieved them from ordering through the catalogs. It seems that Mom and Dad slipped into a routine. They would go to Alliance every week or two, drop off the cream and get the check. That was Mom's money to shop with; Dad would go about doing other ranch business. They would set a time to meet, go buy what few items they needed at the grocery store and then go home.

Aunt Frankie

We received word one day that Mom's older sister, Aunt Frankie, was ill with terminal cancer and wanted to come to be with Mom. It seems that she was somewhat of the "black sheep" of their family and since her husband's death, she was alone and sick. Of course Mom and Dad welcomed her with open arms. She was in pain and mostly bedridden. They fixed a bed in the living room, so Mom would be close by when needed. She lived with them for a few months until the pain became too intense and unbearable. They then moved her to the Alliance hospital where she died a short time later and was buried in the Alliance cemetery. Mom never regretted having her for the short time of at the end of her life.

***

Ranching had become routine. Dad established the Reiger homestead as the summer pasture for the cows and their calves. They were put out to summer pasture around the first of May each year. There they were bred so as to have calves around March and April of the following year. The cattle that Dad had selected to be shipped to market would be put out to pasture on the Bishop homestead range.

Dad would keep up with the market prices, and when he thought prices were at their highest level, it would be time to ship the cattle, usually around October. He would set a shipping date and then order the railroad cars from the train depot in Ellsworth. On the given day, we would gather up the cattle and drive them, by horseback, to Ellsworth and load them on the train. Dad, and sometimes one or two of the older boys, would go with the cattle to the Omaha market where they were sold.

Also in the fall, the calves from the spring would be weaned away from their mothers. They would be the steers that would be shipped the next fall. In the late fall, all the cattle would be brought to the winter pasture. That was a small pasture, but it was between two hay fields making it easier to feed them in the winter months. As the cows got close to having calves, they would be brought in nearer to the ranch barns so they could be watched carefully. Special care had to be given to the small calves to protect them from the cold and from the threat of attacking coyotes.

In the spring, it would be branding time. The neighbors exchanged branding dates and all the cows and calves would be rounded up and brought into the home corral. The calves would be separated from the cows and branded. Dad's brand was called P L open A and looked like this:

It was registered with the state and irons made up. A fire would be built to get the irons red hot, and each calf would be branded on the right back hip. At the same time, the calves would be vaccinated, dehorned and the bull calves would be castrated. Branding day was always a big neighborhood day. The women would cook a big meal and the men would do the branding. Later they would eat dinner and visit. It was a great day to look forward to.

My sister, Helen, met and married Homer Cook in 1930. He was a railroad man who worked on crews that kept the tracks repaired. Being in that business, they were assigned to various towns but eventually settled in Bingham. Through their lives they raised four children.

My brother, Bernie, was born on December 15, 1930. I'm sure Mrs. Thompson was in attendance. It was in the middle of the recession, but it sure didn't slow down the process of having babies.

In 1931, the neighboring boys all decided they wanted rodeo chutes so they could have rodeos on Sundays. So Uncle Floyd, Edson Wilcox, Berl Coe, Homer and Vern built the chutes. They used the chutes for about five years, having rodeos on most Sunday afternoons during the summer months. They used the work horses to ride and also the range cattle. It was another time for the neighbors to meet and visit with each other.

School Teachers

Most of the teachers that taught in the little, one-room schoolhouse were welcomed to the Sandhills and many stayed with our family during their terms. Most were kind and helpful and remained lifelong friends. Rodney tells about one teacher, Harriet Gibbons, and her husband, "Red," who lived on a small ranch nearby. Red would bring her to school on a sled he had rigged up by pulling her and the sled by horseback to school. She was a character, because as he pulled her, she would throw snowballs at him. Rodney hadn't started school yet and sometimes Red would come by our place to visit with Dad. He chewed tobacco and gave Rodney some one day. It made him pretty sick to his stomach.

Ms. Dolphstein was another teacher that stood out as being just the opposite. She was very pushy and had very little patience with kids. She had a way of getting the boys to mind by walking up behind them, picking them up by their ears and shaking them. Duck always had ear trouble and even the wind bothered his ears. One day she picked him up by his ears, shook him and really hurt his ears. Rodney decided it was time to get even so on the way home from school, he found a big sandhill cactus, with lots of stickers on it. He put it in his lunch box and carried it home, took it upstairs and put it in the teacher's bed, underneath the sheet. There were no lights in the bedrooms and you just felt your way when going to bed. Ms. Dolphstein went to bed that night and all of a sudden they heard her scream. She laid down on the cactus. The boys got a big kick out of it, but Mom had a big job of picking the cactus needles out of her backside. Rodney never got in trouble for it because Mom and Dad knew what she was like.

One day at school, Ms. Dolphstein was rough with the girls and was pulling them around by their hair until Homer, being one of the older kids, threatened her with a stove poker. She came home that night and told Mom about it. No doubt Homer had already told Mom about it and an argument ensued. Somehow she got hold of a butcher knife and tried to attach Mom. Homer was there and got the knife away from her. It had become too serious and the school board immediately terminated her and sent her on her way.

Other school teachers during that era were Millie Sowards, who taught one year and then married Edson Wilcox. They stayed in the school district and had children I went to school with. There was also Ima Sheppard who finished teaching one year and taught one full year. She later married Albert Hebbert and they became lifelong friends of Mom and Dad.

Another teacher was Bernard Weekly. He came from Lakeside, was out of work at the time and came to Dad inquiring about teaching. He was hired and, as far as I know, was the only male teacher who ever taught in our district. Mr. Weekly was qualified to teach beyond the eighth grade and talked to Mom and Dad about teaching Rodney and Catherine in ninth grade. He did and they both completed the ninth grade. Catherine went on to graduate from high school, but Rodney talked Mom and Dad into letting him quit school. He said himself that he figured that he knew about all there was to know so he wanted to quit. They let him, although I'm sure they knew he didn't know everything.

ALICE SANDERSON

Winters in the Sandhills were always a concern. With high winds and heavy snow, a severe blizzard could develop in a very short time. Those having to be outdoors to take care of the cattle, and the cattle themselves, were sometimes in danger. The school teacher and the kids going to school had to be aware of blizzard conditions at all times.

One such storm came up in the winter of 1932. The teacher and kids had all gone to school one morning, and around noon time a storm started to form. Alice Sanderson, the teacher, decided to send the kids home. She instructed the older ones to watch out for the younger ones and sent them on their way. In spite of the pleading of the older boys to come with them, she decided to stay awhile, assuring them that she would be along soon. She was staying with our family at the ranch.

She did start out sometime after the kids had left. By that time the winds had picked up and she started drifting with the wind. She soon became hopelessly lost with no idea of where she was. She couldn't stop because of the bitter cold and her only hope was to find her way by accident. Dad knew that she would be in trouble and he sent Vern by horseback to help her home. Vern got to the school, only to find that she had already left. Since the stove was out, that meant she left some time before. He raced back home to tell Dad. With a team of horses pulling a sled and on horseback, Dad, Homer, Vern and a neighbor started out to find her. They searched all over the pasture calling her name, but the wind kept drowning out their voices. With hope fading, they returned to the ranch to regroup and get fresh horses. Dad, thinking it was hopeless finding her alive, due to the cold, sent Homer into Ellsworth to wake the neighbors and get all the help he could to aid in the search.

Everyone was always told that if they became lost, they should never cross a fence, but follow the fence line so they may find their way or be found. Vern and Marvin Ellsberry didn't want to give up and talked Dad into letting them go back out with a team of horses and a sled to try again. They followed the fence line and came across an open gate. There was a hay stack a few feet inside the gate and they decided they would look there. They found her. She had drifted through that open gate, found the hay stack and sat down out of the wind, thinking she was going to die. They put her on the sled and hurried home as fast as they could. By that time, it was early morning and lots of neighbors had gathered to help with the search.

Besides trying to keep her warm, Mom could only think of rubbing snow on the frozen spots, to bring the frost out. A doctor was summoned and when he arrived he said she would have been dead in another 30 minutes. She was extremely lucky as she only lost a few toes on one foot. She recovered and became a lifelong family friend.

That was a very long scary night for everyone. Several gallons of coffee were consumed that night and it was said that Mom and the girls fixed pancake breakfast that morning for twenty-eight men who helped in the search. The people of the sandhills had long lived by helping other people when someone was in trouble.

My sister, Helen, gave birth to their first child on April 24, 1932. It was a boy; the very first grandchild for Mom and Dad. Mom was also pregnant with me. It was said that Dad ran into Emmet Stinnette, a longtime family friend in Alliance. They were visiting and Emmett said, "Gee Paul, with all those kids it must be getting difficult to think up names for the new ones." Dad said, "Yes it is hard. We have thirteen now and expecting another, but we haven't had to name one Emmett yet!"

THE CABOOSE

It was a bright sunny morning in the Sandhills; a slight breeze was blowing like it always does. My Dad and brothers were out milking the cows and feeding the pigs and chickens. My sisters were in the house getting breakfast started. It was about 6 A.M. and everyone was doing their usual thing for that time of the morning. There was something different about this morning, however. Mom was about to have another baby. Mrs. Thompson had been called in a few days earlier to help. It certainly wasn't new to Mom and Dad. They had delivered thirteen other children very nearly the same way.

My Dad and brothers finished the chores and came into the house to eat breakfast. My sisters were ready and they all sat down to eat. Just after they got started, Mrs. Thompson opened the bedroom door and called my Dad. He went into the bedroom and after a few minutes everyone heard a baby cry. Everyone finished eating except Dad, but nobody left the table. Finally Dad came out, never said anything, and finished eating his breakfast. He was always good at that. He would just leaving you hanging until he was ready to tell you. Finally, after finishing eating, he said, "It's a boy." I don't know if it was ever discussed, but I suspect it was. Mom and Dad had thirteen other kids, seven girls and six boys. So when I came into the world as "it's a boy," that made it even: seven girls and seven boys and a total of fourteen.

I don't know what happened, but that was the end of a long line of kids. Dad always referred to me as the caboose. Maybe they had it planned that way or maybe they just took one look at me and said, "That's it, no more."

There was a rodeo planned in Lakeside that Fourth of July. Dad and all the kids went. I guess it was the time they told all the neighbors about me. It must have been a banner day for Rodney. He won $2 on the bareback horse riding contest and $1 in the Shetland pony riding race. Rodney and the other older boys were becoming pretty good "cowboys." Rodney told of one time that a man from around there wanted 700 cows and calves driven to Brownlee, Nebraska some 150 miles to the east. Duck and Rodney took the job. It took them three weeks, but they earned $1 a day and thought it was great.

My brother, Homer, married Betty Thompson in 1933. It was decided at the time that he would stay on the ranch and work for Dad. They built a small house across the lake from the ranch house, a small barn and sod milk house. Homer and Betty lived there for a few years before moving to another ranch some five miles from Mom and Dad's. They later moved to Idaho to establish their own place. For many years after that, Homer always sent Mom and Dad a fresh cut pine tree for Christmas. He would cut it, wrap it in wet burlap and ship it by train to Ellsworth. It really made our Christmas's brighter. Through their lives, Homer and Betty raised three children.

The years between birth and five years old, when you could start remembering, could best be described as the molding years. That is molding into the family. There were lots of kids and it was always family and chores. My brother, Bernie, is one and a half years older than I am, and sister Phyllis is a year and a month older than he is. Sister Lois was a year and half older than her, and brother Jim was a year and a half older than her; and so it went throughout the family. There are twenty and a half years between my oldest sister Helen and me. So there was always family, small ones to play with and the older ones to look up to. There is no doubt that the older ones helped raise the younger ones. There is no doubt that we all got into trouble at times and also that I was somewhat spoiled. I guess, being the youngest, made me that way.

Mom usually handled the small problems that came up, but when it got severe she would say, "Just wait until your father hears about this." Look out because that was bad news. Dad never beat any of us, but when we needed a swat to get our attention, we got it. Mom could be tough, too. I will never forget her saying, "I don't know much about raising kids, but I do know that when it comes to kids, someone has to be boss." And she was the boss when she had to be.

***

No major illnesses gave the family a scare like the small pox epidemic that almost claimed Mom's life in 1921, but there were two accidents and one serious illness that caused grave concern. Mom always paid particular attention to providing a balanced diet. That probably had a lot to do with the general good health of our family. In approximately 1930, Marjorie was about eight years old when her leg was severely injured in an accident. Helen was driving the touring car into the garage, just before a rain storm and Marjorie jumped on the running board to ride. Not knowing she was there, Helen got too close to the side of the garage door frame and Marjorie's leg got caught at the calf and it was ripped, nearly to the bone, down to her ankle. She spent many months under a doctor's care, in a special chair and it miraculously healed without a limp. She always had a terrible scar on the back of that leg.

During the winter of 1932, Catherine dressed for school in a long wool stocking and came downstairs to her breakfast. While she was standing next to the stove, Mom removed a pan of hot grease and accidentally dropped it, spilling down Catherine's leg. When they took off the stocking , the burned flesh came off with it. It took months for it to heal and before it did, she was kicked by a cow, on that same leg. She always had the imprint of a cow hoof in the scar on her leg.

In approximately 1935, Rodney woke up one Sunday morning with a stomach ache. Mom, thinking it was a simple stomach ache, told him to stay in bed. That night it let up and he fell asleep. The next morning he woke up with a very high fever. Mom and Dad rushed him to the hospital in Alliance. His appendix had ruptured. They had to drain the poison off and it took several weeks for him to recover.

***

My sister, Margaret, married Russell Enright in 1934. During the 1940s, they separated and divorced. Margaret married Bob Huddle in 1949 and moved to California where they finished raising the four boys from Margaret's first marriage.

Dad had a tradition that when one of us kids turned five years old, for their birthday he would build them their very own milk stool for their birthday. The stool consisted of a board nailed across a piece of sawed-off fence post and braced a couple of times. I can remember when I first got mine. I thought it was great because it meant I could work with the older kids.

EDUCATION

Being five years old also meant going to school. It was a one-room school with a single teacher who taught all eight grades. All my older brothers and sisters had attended the same school. Jim, Lois, Phyllis, Bernie and I would all head out to school about 7:30 A.M. Mom packed us all a lunch. Off we would go through the yard, past the root cellar and chicken pen and over a wood gate into the pasture. We would walk up over the hills, past blow outs and over a small hill to the schoolhouse.

It was a small stucco building no more than twenty-five feet long and twenty feet wide. It had a front porch and a small entry room where we all hung our coats. There was a wood burning stove that was used to heat the room; the schoolyard had a water pitcher pump where we drew out water. The "privies" were In back of the schoolhouse, one for the girls and one for the boys. There was a small shed and pen for those that rode horses to school. Oh how we use to envy them because we had to walk. Dad said that they had farther to come and we could easily walk the distance.

We had all the necessities; now it was time to learn. There was reading, writing and arithmetic. We also had spelling, history and geography in different grades. The teacher would spend about fifteen minutes with each grade in each subject. The rest of the time we sat and studied. There was a fifteen-minute recess during mid-morning, a thirty-minute lunch break at noon and another recess in the afternoon. During the breaks, we would play ball if the weather was nice; in the winter we would sleigh ride on the hills by the schoolhouse. It would then be 4 P.M. and it was time to go home and get our chores started.

Education was very important to Mom. She always said "There was no excuse for anyone to not read and learn all of their lives." All of the family graduated from the eighth grade in that small stucco schoolhouse. Due to the demand of ranch work, Homer and Vern were not able to go on to high school. Helen went to Alliance and graduated from high school. Margaret went to Scottsbluff for one year and then to Alliance for the remainder of high school. Duck took correspondence courses for some two years.

Higher education was not out of the grasp of some of the girls. Helen and Catherine went on to nurses training at the Alliance hospital. Marjorie went to junior college in Scottsbluff and worked in stenography and business for a few years. Lois and Phyllis both went to Chadron, Nebraska to college and became teachers. Phyllis taught one year at the one room schoolhouse from which she graduated.

Sometime during the mid to late 1930s, Helen and Homer were living in Bingham where there was a high school. They decided if Dad would build them a house to live in, the rest of the kids could board with them and finish high school. Dad bought an old store building, tore it down, and built the house. Catherine, Marjorie, Jean, Lois and Phyllis all graduated from the Bingham High School. Sometime in the early 1940s, they opened a state agriculture high school in Curtis, Nebraska. Jim, Bernie and I went one year to Bingham and then transferred to Curtis and graduated from high school there.

6. GROWING UP

Growing up on the ranch would seem pretty routine, but I got into my share of trouble. It was mostly kid stuff, but I'm sure it was enough to drive my Mom and Dad crazy. I guess that's what kids are for: to test the patience of their parents to see how much they can get away with. Between the ages of five to ten, I managed to do some pretty crazy things.

There was a time around 1937 that Mom and Dad were going to Bingham to see Helen and I wanted to go. Mom said no, I was to stay home with the older girls. That made me mad and I was determined to go anyway, so I hid in the back seat of the car. Dad, not seeing me, even opened the back door and put a shovel on the seat. After leaving, we hit a bump going into Ellsworth, causing the shovel to bounce up and hit me on the leg. I yelled "ouch." They heard me and, of course, I was discovered. I didn't know what was going to happen. There was a long pause and finally Dad started laughing. At that time I knew that I was going to get my way.

Another time in 1937, we were all going to Sunday School at a neighbor's house. Mom had dressed Bernie and me and we were out playing in the yard. Dad was having problems with the Delco plant that provided our power for lights and had been working on it. It was in the milk house and he came out to get ready to go to Sunday School. Before going into the house he told us, "Don't you kids go in the milk house and touch those two bare wires together because if you do, it will blow up the batteries." There were thirty-six glass batteries that provided the electricity for the place. I never did understand why Dad always had to explain everything to us, but that was just his way. I'm sure it wasn't intended to cause us any harm, but to explain that to a couple of kids is like inviting them to try it. Anyway, he no more than got in the house and we headed for the milk house. Sure enough, there was two bare wires hanging there. Bernie was by the door and he kept telling me not to do it, but I just had to find out. So I touched the wires. It blew up six of the glass batteries. Glass flew all over and we got drenched in acid water. It was a wonder we weren't killed. We immediately got a baking soda bath, and we still went to Sunday School.

Around that same time, we were all in the house because it was a bitter cold day, somewhere around 40 degrees below zero. Dad was working on something and needed a hammer. He said to Bernie, "Put your coat on and go to the garage and get the claw hammer. Don't stick your tongue on the hammer because it's frosted and if you do, your tongue will stick to the hammer." Off Bernie went and sure enough he stuck his tongue on the hammer. Next he got worried because he was afraid of what Dad would say, so he jerked the hammer down and took a layer of skin off his tongue. It bled a lot and he was crying, but I thought it was pretty funny because he was the one in trouble for a change.

My sister, Phyllis, tells of the time when she was five years old and Jim was giving her a ride around the barn on our pony, Polo. Jim was leading Polo when the pony stepped on a tin can and moved sideways. This caused Phyllis to fall off and break her arm. Jim got a spanking for being careless and Mom and Dad had to take Phyllis to the doctor to get her arm set.

Phyllis also told of the time when she was in the second grade. Gene Wilcox, a neighbor boy, rode his pony, Buck, to school. Phyllis had a "crush" on Gene and evidently the feeling was mutual. After school, Gene asked Phyllis to take a ride on Buck. Phyllis was impressed and said she would. Dad was at the school working on the water pitcher pump that had broken. When Phyllis got on Buck, he started running and bucking. Phyllis started screaming, "Buck, Buck, Buck." Finally the pony threw her off and she hit the ground on her rear end. She got up totally humiliated. Dad looked at her and said, "You were yelling Buck. What did you think he was doing?" That was the end of their crushes on each other.

Rodney was always teasing us. Once, when I was about five years old, I woke up and went downstairs to put on my shoes and socks. I was sitting on the kitchen floor; Mom was fixing breakfast. Rodney said, "Don, make sure you put those socks on the right foot because if you don't you will get 'pigeon toed.'" I would start and he would say, "No, no, not that foot." I kept changing and he kept saying it. Finally Mom said, "Rodney, quit teasing that kid." Then I knew he was just teasing. I still looked up to him even when he teased me.

Don, with Sadie and Hot Shot, her colt.

Working in the hay fields in the summer was very dirty work. You would sweat and the dust would stick right to your skin. My brother, Vern, devised a shower in the milk house. He built a bracket and put a fifty gallon barrel up on it. The sun would heat the water during the day and he rigged up a shower head so you could take showers. One afternoon all the girls decided they would go to the milk house and take a shower. Bernie and I were nearby playing, and I decided I should see what the girls were doing; so I opened the door. They were naked. I learned very quickly that wasn't the thing to do. When they told Mom about it, I got a pretty severe spanking.

Mom made almost all of our clothing. The only things that were bought were overalls for the boys and Dad and shoes. Not only did she sew all of the dresses, skirts and shirts, but also the underwear. She taught all of the girls to sew and besides their other chores, they were always sewing. They bought the yearly supply of flour in 100-pound bags, usually several at a time. The

Our first family photo, 1937: Standing, from left, Marjorie, Vern, Catherine, Rodney, Helen and Homer. Front, from left, Phyllis, Margeret, Dad, Bernie (on lap), Lois, Mom, Don (on lap) and Duck.

bags were made of a cotton material with a flower or other design on it. Mom and the girls would make clothes out of them. They also made bed sheets, pillowcases and dish towels. A lot of times you could see brand names such as "Mother Knows Best" or "Gooches Best" imprinted on our sheets, towels and underwear.

Around this time, our pony, Polo, died of old age and Dad bought another pony we named "Sadie." Dad bought her from a man named Gene Crosser. When he brought her out to the ranch, he took the back seat out of a sedan car and led her in. That was about the right height for her. She became my boyhood friend. There was only one problem: she had to be kept in the boarded calves pen. When she was loose, she would climb through barb wire fences to be with the other horses.

Dad bought a new Plymouth in 1937, so Mom and Dad decided they would take a trip to Indiana to see Granddad Dwiggins. They took Bernie and me with them. That was the only time I ever saw my Granddad Dwiggins. While I don't remember all of it, I do remember that he had a small apple orchard, which Mom told us not to go near. While we were visiting, Granddad took us there and gave us each an apple. I also remember seeing the aunts and uncles on my mother's side.

We also had our first family picture taken in 1937. Homer and Betty had come home from Idaho and it was the first opportunity to have us all together. Mom was always a great one to get all the family together.

In the late 1930s, the government had a project to plant trees for soil conservation, as they felt the trees would hold the soil. Dad put them in a "shelter belt" in the home meadow. It was ten rows of different kinds of trees that ran along the north and east side of the meadows. It was about a mile long and there were a lot of weeds that needed hoeing. It also provided pig weeds for the pigs and a haven for pheasants and grouse that we hunted all through the 1940s.

The trees provided a lot of work that kept us out of mischief. At least once or twice a year, Dad had us hoe the weeds so they wouldn't kill the small tree plants. That went on for several years, until the trees got big enough to survive with the weeds. The weeds would grow into seed, which was good feed for the wild birds. I remember when some of the trees got caterpillar worms all over them. Dad had us take a can of kerosene and go through the trees picking off the worms and putting them in the kerosene to kill them.

We also had a lot of fun. I remember ice skating on the lake that was close to the house. It was an alkali lake and the muskrats used to thrive in it. They would build houses out of "bull rushes" to get out of the water and, in the winter, when the water froze, the tops of their houses which stuck up above the ice, made seats for us to sit on while we were resting after skating. Besides sledding on the hills, every spare minute we could find we would be ice skating.

Whenever there was ice available, especially on the holidays, Mom would make ice cream. What a treat that was! They had an ice cream maker that you turned by hand. We would crush the ice, pour it down around the ice cream canister and turn it until it made the mixture into ice cream. You never heard any of us kids complain about having to do that.

I remember our neighbor, Ralph Munger, coming to the house. He always had something to say about us. Lois always liked to talk and Ralph called her "chatterbox"; Phyllis was kind of chubby and he called her "fat." I weighed twelve pounds when I was born and he always said that, "I had gained a pound and lost a pound since." I was kind of skinny then. The Mungers were excellent neighbors.

One Sunday when we were having Sunday School at our place, Shorty and Mrs. Thompson were the first ones to arrive. Dad, Shorty and I were sitting in the living room visiting. We had just had a bad storm. Shorty said that once during a storm he tied down a log chain by hooking it around a tree. He later went into the house and was looking out the window at that log chain, the wind blowing it straight out, whipping so hard that the chain links were popping off the end. Dad shook his head in agreement, but I don't think he believed it. Dad always said, "Shorty never lied, but he did stretch the truth a lot."

During this time, my brother Duck was in the barn shoveling manure onto the manure spreader. Jim and our cousin, Ray Dwiggins, were supposed to be helping him, but they disappeared. He found find them upstairs in Vern and Rodney's bedroom. They had found some chewing tobacco and were chewing and spitting it all around the room. Duck started chasing them. They ran out through the barn, through the hay loft, jumped into the barnyard and headed out to the Mungers, our neighbors. When Mom came home, she stopped at the Mungers and brought them home. When she found out what they had done, she made them scrub the room, with hand brushes, on their hands and knees, until it was all cleaned up.

I'm not sure where Dad acquired it, but he had a 12-gauge shotgun with a long barrel that we used for hunting. It had been used so much, the end was worn and it would spray the pellets of a shotgun shell in a wide pattern. The wood fore grip had gotten lost and how that gun kicked. We called it "Long Tom." If you just pointed that gun at something and fired, enough pellets sprayed out to hit something. We used to hunt through the shelter belt with that gun and almost always came home with some birds. We also used it for hunting ducks on the lake. After eating chicken, beef and pork, the wild birds were really a treat. Mom usually made that our special Sunday dinner.

Going to Bingham to stay for a week or so with my sister

Helen and her family was a big treat for me. Her son, Melvin, who was my older nephew by two months, and I used to have great fun playing and going Bull-head fishing. Once we caught more than Helen could use for sup-per, so we cleaned

Phyllis and Lois herding turkeys.

them and went around town selling them for a nickel each. One time we had some pennies that we took to the railroad tracks, about 100 feet from Helen's house, and put them on the track. When a train came through, it flattened them. Then we would have to look for half a day to find them. At least we thought we were having fun.

On one of those trips to Helen's, one of her neighbors, the Wilders, gave me a pair of tame ducks. I took them to the ranch where I thought I was going to start raising ducks. They were there for some time. I fed them and my imagination grew rampant that I was going to be a big duck grower. One Sunday morning, Bernie saw them sitting on the lake and, thinking they were wild ducks, crept on his hands and knees for a long way along the rushes with old "Long Tom." He raised up and killed them both with one shot. That was the end of my imaginative duck raising. We ate them that day for our dinner.

Between 1939 to 1941, the Sandhills experienced a siege of grasshoppers. They are leaping, plant-eating, orthopteran insects that were ravaging and destroying the hay fields. At the same time, the Alliance creamery was hatching turkeys in the spring of the year, with the thought of feeding and having them ready for the holidays. They would offer them to farmers and ranchers to raise for a profit. Dad got the idea that if he took the turkeys, we could take them out through the hay fields where they could feed on grasshoppers. It was an ingenious idea because it not only fed the turkeys, but it saved the hay fields.

TURKEYS

Dad built ten pens, side by side, and a shed, all with straw roofs, just in front of our house. Initially, Dad got the turkeys at no cost from the creamery. He would start the turkeys under kerosene brooders when he first got them. As they grew into young turkeys, they would even have to be taught how to roost. Turkeys are not known for being too smart. As they grew, it was time to start taking them out through the hay fields. They always had to have water mid-morning and in the afternoons which was delivered by horse and wagon by one of the older boys. Generally the herding was done by Lois, Phyllis, Bernie and me. Because the turkeys weren't too smart, they were scared to death of the burlap bag we used to herd them.

I remember Adolph, a dog we had who used to be with us when we herded the turkeys. He was mostly mongrel, but at least part Collie. He was a good dog and my brother Duck always called him "Dolphy." One day when they were out herding the turkeys with Adolph, a severe storm came up; they left Adolph and the turkeys at the little place across the lake and headed home. After the storm blew over, Mom told us to go and bring home the turkeys. As we got closer, we saw Dolphy walking back and forth behind the turkeys, herding them home.

I remember one other time during a bad storm. Dad and the older boys were in the hay field when a cyclone formed over the lake and headed straight for our house. You could see the funnel shape and Mom started yelling for us to head for the root cellar. We all got into the cellar and the storm was throwing water and mud all over the place but as it approached, it just as suddenly turned and went in a different direction.

Around Thanksgiving, Dad would sell the turkeys back to the creamery for $1 each. For herding the turkeys, Dad would give each of us $5 to spend on Christmas. We thought we were really rich.

Later, Dad started keeping 100 hen and ten tom turkeys. He would feed them laying mash so they would lay eggs. We would gather the eggs, clean them, pack them in crates and Dad would sell them to the creamery for hatching. As I recall, this went on through the war years.

It seems that I still had an impulse to get into trouble. I remember a time when Mom and Dad were going to Alliance and I wanted to go. They said absolutely not and was I ever mad. I was out in the barn where there was a chicken walking around. Dad had dropped an ear of corn that he fed to the pigs. I picked it up and threw it as hard as I could at the chicken. It hit it right on the head and it flopped down. Thinking that I had killed it, I hid it under some hay. When I got over being mad, I thought I better bury that chicken before Dad found it and I'd be in more trouble. I got a shovel and went to get the chicken. I looked under the hay where I'd put it, but it was gone. I guess I just knocked it out. That was a relief!

My brother, Rodney, married Mildred Brammer in 1939. They were married at her home in Bingham. It made me mad at the time because they thought Bernie and I were too young to attend. We got over it. During their lives they raised four children.

My sister, Catherine, married Leslie Hulshirer in 1939. They were later divorced and she married T. J. Halkins in 1945. She had two children by her first husband and two with T.J.

My brother, Vern, married Maudie Keller in 1940. They moved into the little house across the lake where they lived for a few years until they leased a ranch five miles north and started ranching there. They later sold out and moved to Chadron, Nebraska. Through their lives they raised four children.

Dad always gave the boys our haircuts, but when Vern got married, he inherited the job. I remember the times Bernie and I would walk to their place across the lake to get our hair cut. He used squeeze clippers, and occasionally a hair would get caught which hurt, but you didn't dare complain too much.

7. The War Years

With World War II raging, it again became a very scary time. With the memory of World War I still on everyone's mind, the bombing of Pearl Harbor brought its fury of war and threat of death. My brother, Duck, was drafted first. He initially was assigned to the cavalry in Fort Robinson, close to home. He was later transferred to the infantry and, for most of the war, served in New Guinea in the Pacific. He was never wounded, but he caught malaria and it affected him all his life.

My brother, Jim, was drafted next and, after training, sent to Germany. He probably had the roughest part of it all. He spent his entire time on the front lines and saw considerable combat action. At the end of the war, he came home on thirty days leave and was working in the hay field when the Ellsworth Depot agent came with a telegram telling him the war with Japan was over and for him to report to a base in Missouri for discharge. After his leave, he was scheduled to go to the Pacific to finish out the war. I shall never forget the expression on his face when he got the news of peace. He was only eighteen years old when he was drafted, barely past being a kid himself. Put into war requires one to grow up fast. Let there be no mistake about it: *WAR IS HELL*.

My brother, Rodney, also was drafted, but because he was married and because it was later in the war years, he never had to leave the United States. Uncle Cecil and Uncle Kenneth also were drafted and they both spent their military service time in Europe.

War is devastating to families. There is always the fear of getting word that someone had been killed in action. Our immediate family was very fortunate and all my brothers came home safely. Two of our aunts and uncles were not so fortunate. Aunt

Iva and Uncle Dave lost their son, Junior, in Okinawa, and Aunt Edith and Uncle Charlie lost their son, Keith, in combat in North Africa. We must never forget those who paid the supreme price by giving their lives for our country.

My sister, Margaret, was having marital problems and she and her husband got divorced, leaving her with five small children to care for. It was impossible to do. My brother, Vern, and his wife, Maudie, adopted the one girl. The four boys, Randall, Buddy, Paul, and Jack, came to live with Mom and Dad. Jack was just a one or two years old at the time; it must have been like starting over again to Mom and Dad. Randall and Bud fit right in and started going to school with us. I don't know how Paul got the nickname "Pork," but it always stuck. Jack was a little tyke, with blonde curly hair. I can still see Dad scooping him up after supper, putting him on his lap and giving him his pocket watch to play with, while he read the paper.

Life on the ranch during the war years was different, as we all had to do the work of those who had gone into the service and, at the same time, worry about their well-being. I know that Mom and Dad worried a lot. Dad hired a man named Fred Sidow to help with the ranch work. Sometime around then, Bernie and I had picked up the habit of smoking, much to Mom's dismay. We used to sneak around, out of Mom's sight to smoke, because if we got caught, we would get a spanking. Old Fred would get cigarettes for us. I'm sure Mom and Dad never knew that, or they would have fired him.

I remember once Mom caught Bernie smoking in the outside privy. She told him he had to tell Dad he had been smoking or she was going to and it would be worse. Bernie waited until Dad was in the bathroom shaving that day when he told him. Since Dad was busy shaving, Bernie figured he could sneak out. He started, but Dad stopped him and told him to wait right where he was. I'm sure the wait was worse than the punishment. When Dad finished shaving, Bernie got a couple of licks with Dad's razor strap.

My sister, Jean, tells of the time during the war years when she asked Mom if she could join the WACs. Mom was adamant in telling her that she couldn't. According to my sister, Mom said,

"Nice girls don't do that." I have no idea why she would think it wouldn't be for nice girls. I feel that Jean thought as I did. I was always in awe of the guys in uniforms and wanted to serve also. The government built an Army/Air Force base in Alliance where they trained men as paratroopers and

Duck, after being drafted and assigned to Fort Robinson.

glider pilots. Some of the girls got to know some of the boys who were in training and would ask them down to the ranch. Dad would go to the base, pick them up and bring them to the ranch for a weekend. It was great for them and for us. Since we couldn't have our own brothers with us, at least we could talk to someone else's brother.

My sister, Lois, was going with one of the boys from the base and, I guess, it was pretty serious. Just after D-Day, she got a letter from the boy's mother telling her he had been killed in action during the D-Day jump in France.

Once during that time, a plane, with a glider in tow, was on a training flight over the sandhills when they developed some kind of trouble. In order to save the airplane, they had to cut the glider loose and it landed in a meadow just north of the ranch. They had Military Police guarding it, but you could go see it. I remember Dad taking all the small kids to see it. It was very impressive.

I also remember all the things that were rationed, like gas, tires and sugar. There were others, but those were the only ones Mom and Dad talked about. Mom was worried about the sugar because she canned so much. Dad was concerned about the gas and tires because of having to get the cream and eggs to market. Dad always followed the thirty-five miles-per-hour speed limit that was imposed to save on gas mileage. It seemed that it took forever to get to Alliance. I remember the song, *"Rosie the Riveter,"* a tribute to the women

From lett, Margaret's boys, Randall, Pork, Brother Jim holding Jackie, and Buddie.

that went to work in the factories to manufacture the goods the men needed to fight the war. All in all, I don't believe that the rationing bothered the ranch too much and we got through it.

I remember when the war was over in Europe. We heard it on the radio and listened to the big celebration they were having in New York City. I also remember when the war was over in the Pacific. Those were big nights for the family.

Of course, all through the war years, school was always there. As in the past, most of the teachers stayed, at least through the week, at our place.

My sister, Marjorie, married Glenn Keller in 1943. He was a brother to Vern's wife, Maudie. During their lifetime, they raised two children. After the death of her husband, Marjorie married Ed Frueling in 1985.

My sister, Jean, married Harvey Plaster also in 1943. They raised five children.

All of the people in the Sandhills shipped their cattle to market through the Ellsworth stockyard. The ranchers who lived far north of our place couldn't drive the cattle to Ellsworth in one day; they often would come as far as our place, spend the night and go on the next day. Dad would have them put their cattle in

Above, from left are all the kids who went to school in 1943: Bud Enright, Glen Munger, Randall Enright, Don Lineback, Della Munger, Bill Munger, Bernie and Phyllis Lineback. At right are Phyllis, Bernie and Don. Both photos taken on the schoolhouse steps.

the quarter section just south of the home meadow and Mom would fix them supper and breakfast. They always paid Mom a few dollars, but it wasn't much; it was more of a neighborly thing to do. Sometimes Bernie and I would ride with them, helping to drive the cattle. One time we were helping a rancher named Ed Pisel. We just finished driving the cattle through an open gate and Ed got off his horse to close the gate. He sneezed and his upper false teeth came out and landed in a big pile of fresh cow manure. Ed just reached down, picked up his teeth, wrapped them in his handkerchief and, when we got to the next horse tank, rinsed them off and put them back in his mouth. All of the ranchers would give us a dollar when we got to Ellsworth. We could buy a lot of cigarettes for a dollar.

All through those years, we had a lot of cousins who came to visit us on the ranch. It was always great fun. We always called them our "city cousins." Of course we thought we knew everything and used to laugh at them when they would try to ride a horse or milk a cow. We used to play tricks on them by taking them "snipe" hunting. We gave them a burlap bag with a few kernels of corn in it and took them out to the hills, telling them to sit there with the bag open. The snipes would come to get the

Jackie in the turkey pen (circa. 1942).

corn and they then could catch them. We would go back to the house and wait to see how long they would wait before coming home. They usually ended up being mad at us for a little while.

Two of our "city cousins" immediately come to mind. Aunt Hazel had four kids.

Jim and Mary, the two middle ones, were at the ranch almost every summer for most of their teen years. They fit right in. Jim helped in the hay field and Mary helped with the housework. Mary tells of the time she was with Dad when he got the pickup stuck in the sand. She said he just got out, lit his pipe and said, "Mary Louise, we're stuck." She couldn't get over how unemotional he was. That was just Dad's way. She also told about the time when Mom made a batch of bread which, for some reason, didn't turn out right. She told the kids, including Mary, to take and feed it to the pigs. We started to do that, but then decided to toss it around like a football. Mom caught us and made us stop. It just shows that we could play with almost anything.

During those years they began having dances at the Ellsworth schoolhouse. It was a good-size building, about twenty feet by thirty feet with a full basement. The dancing would be upstairs; the neighbor ladies would fix food and coffee downstairs. It was during a dance in Ellsworth when my brother, Jim, came home from the war. He had come by ship to New York City, took a train to Alliance and hitchhiked to Ellsworth. None of us knew that he was coming because he didn't know himself. He just walked in. That was a pleasant shock to everyone.

8. AFTER THE WAR

After the war, all of the men came home. Duck came home and worked at the ranch for awhile, as did my brother, Jim. Shortly after their return, a trade school opened in the eastern part of Nebraska. War veterans could go there on their G.I. Bill and receive training in various trades. Duck and Jim both went; Duck for Equipment Operator and Jim for Big Motor Maintenance. They worked in those fields most of their adult lives.

Uncle Cecil came home and was at the ranch for awhile. He later had a small farm in Lemoyne, Nebraska, near Uncle Merle. Uncle Kenneth, who somehow got the nickname "Huck," came home to the ranch for awhile and spent the rest of his life working on the various big ranches around the Sandhills. My brother, Rodney, who was married before he went in the service, returned home to his family. We were all together again and ready to get on with life.

Purchasing any kind of vehicle was impossible during the war. Dad bought a new Plymouth pickup in 1945. That was a big boost for the ranch work and it was special for me because I learned to drive with it. Dad bought a new Plymouth sedan car in 1946. That year was also the year I graduated from the eighth grade and the schoolhouse. There was just Mom, Dad and I at home.

I remember that year well because Dad was milking twenty cows which had to be done morning and night. It was just the two of us to do it. I would get started about 5:30 A.M. Around seven, Dad would say, "You better get in the house, eat breakfast and get ready for school." When I got home from school, it was time to start the chores over again. It usually took us about two hours to complete the chores each time. Then I thought I would

The "Ranch" in 1946.

really appreciate going away to school the next year. In later years, Mom and Dad would be there alone. Either one of the boys would be home or Dad would hire a man to help him.

Winters consisted of going to school;, the summers consisted of working the ranch. Early in the spring there were fences to be mended. We would take a wagon load of new fence posts, extra wire, shovel, hammer and staples, and with one driving and one walking, we would follow the fence line checking for rotten posts and broken wires. Sometimes winters raised havoc with the fences. Then it would be branding time and getting the cattle ready for summer pasture. All the windmills had to be checked to make sure they were operating to ensure the water supply for the cattle.

After the war ended, Dad was having trouble with the water storage tank. It was old and beginning to leak. The tank was about ten feet above ground level and wasn't high enough to provide much water pressure in the house. There was a hill just west of the barnyard, probably 200 feet high, and Dad thought if he could build a cistern tank on top of that hill and a windmill to pump water, he could greatly improve the system. It was a big undertaking, but he decided to try it.

First, a trench was dug in a circle, probably ten feet in diameter, about five feet deep and filled with concrete. A concrete cover was made with an opening so they could get in; then they started digging out the dirt. When they got close to the five feet level, they went down another five feet and dug the sand out of that. A concrete bottom was put in and the cistern was done. Dad's neighbor, who drilled wells for a living, came and drilled a well from the top of the hill. I remember Dad saying he was surprised they struck water at about forty feet when the hill was

Windmill on Buck Brush Hill, built 1945.

about 200 feet above ground level.

With the well and cistern done, it was time to lay the pipe to the house. That was a big job because the sides kept caving while digging the trench. Uncle Huck who was there helping, did much of that project. As far as I know, that was the first time we ever had an outside water faucet and Dad put that one by his garden. It really improved the water pressure inside the house.

Branding time was always the spring highlight for us. It was not only our own branding, but all of the neighbors who traded branding days. Branding would go on for a month or more. We rounded up the cattle, brought them into the home place, separated the calves from their mothers and then began the branding. Everyone would be assigned a job to do: someone vaccinated, someone dehorned the calves, someone castrated the bull calves, and someone branded. Usually it was the kids' job to hold the calves down while everything was being done. Calves testicles are really good to eat. Mom would never allow us to bring them in the house, so we would wash them in the tank, string them on a piece of number nine wire and roast them over the branding fire.

Sometime during this period, Dad gave each of us a heifer (female calf) to start our own cattle herd. We all got brands that were registered with the state.

Soon haying season would be starting and we would have to get the machinery ready to go. Dad was very carefully checked every piece of equipment to be sure it was in top shape. He never wanted to have a breakdown that would cause a delay in the haying. On rainy days, we would take the horses harnesses upstairs to the hayloft, hang them over the stair loft railings, and oil the leather straps and repair any damage. After July 4, the haying season would begin in earnest. We always got up early, but it seemed even

Jim and Dad working cattle.

earlier in haying season. After the chores, we would be through with breakfast and ready for work by 7 A.M. One of us would go wrangle the horses.

If it was a mowing day, Dad would start sharpening the sickle blades. He had a whet stone, behind the garage, which was run by a small electric motor. It had to be wet to grind the cycle blade, so he rigged up a gallon tin can with a hole in the bottom, that trickle water onto the stone while he sharpened each blade. Each mower had a freshly sharpened blade each day and he always carried two extra blades in case one broke during the day. On mowing days, it was almost always my job to rake the hay into winrows. Generally, we would mow one day and sweep and stack the next. Depending how heavy the grass was, we would put up two or three stacks in a day.

On those days it was my job to "scatter rake," which was raking up after Dad swept the hay. There was always some hay that dribbled off and Dad never wasted anything. In the early times, haying was done entirely by teams of horses but around 1947, Dad bought a Ford tractor. He used it for both mowing and sweeping the hay. It really sped up the haying season.

I do remember one time, though, that I didn't get much accomplished. Dad sent me with the tractor to mow the old homestead meadow. Thinking that a tractor with all that power would go any place, I drove it too close to the alkali lake and buried it in mud. I tried to get it out all day, but to no avail and ended up walking home to tell Dad. They were haying in the home meadow.

1947 Family Portrait: Standing from left, Margaret, Phyllis, Lois, Rodney, Duck, Helen, Marjorie, Bernie and Jim. Seated from left, Don, Catherine, Vern, Mom, Dad, Jean and Homer.

They stopped what they were doing and Dad took a team of four horses and a log chain and we went back and pulled out the tractor. Dad explained a few things about alkali mud to me that day.

We still had visits from our city cousins. It didn't make much difference to Mom and Dad if you were there, because you would have work to do. After the haying, it would be back to school. I remember those days well and while we were always busy, it was a good life and we did enjoy ourselves.

Just after the war they built a big Quonset hut dance hall in Ashby, Nebraska. It seemed there were several big bands who would travel by bus around the country playing at dances. They used to have dances in Ashby every other Saturday in the summertime. Vern and Maudie almost always went and all the kids would go with them. Marjorie and Glenn, who at the time lived on a ranch north of Ashby, would also go. Mom always said that as long as we were with the older ones, she didn't worry. If she only knew some of the things we did, like getting some beer, she wouldn't have said that. It was great fun during those summers.

Sometimes when Dad was shipping cattle and going with

them to Omaha, he would bring us a present. He always brought Mom something and, when we were young, he would bring us a toy or some store bought clothes. One time when Pork and Jack were there, Dad bought each one of them a pair of khaki colored jeans. They thought that they were great because they had pockets. The girls always said they almost had to catch Jack to get his off to wash. He called them his "hip pockets."

We had our second family picture taken in June 1947. What an affair that was. Mom was always great for that. It didn't make any difference how many people were there, how she was going to feed them or where they were going to sleep. She wrote to all the relations and invited them. I think that the majority came because we had people all over the place. As usual there was enough food and we ate in shifts. She started getting ready for the big meal at least three days before, baking pies and getting the meats lined up. Everyone was on their own for sleeping arrangements.

Most of the adults got the beds and the kids were sent to the hay loft to sleep. Hay doesn't make a bad bed. Some people came just for the day of the reunion. The total count that day was well over a hundred. Like the time before, Mr. Worley came from his studio in Alliance to take the family picture.

My brother, Jim, married Fern Taylor in 1947. During their marriage they had three children. They later divorced and Jim remarried.

My sister, Lois, married Bill Keller in 1948. He is a cousin of Vern's wife and Marjorie's husband. During their lives together, they raised three children.

During the 1948-49 school year, my sister, Lois, was teaching school in our home district. During the blizzard of '49, and because only Pork and Jack were going to school at the time, Dad decided that they could hold school in our ranch house for the remainder of that year. My sister, Phyllis, was there to teach. They just cleaned out one of the upstairs bedrooms and made it into a school. That was the last year they held school in the little stucco schoolhouse.

During that year, Mom and Dad began thinking of retiring. That was a big step for them. All their friends were in the sandhills, but the kids were all growing up and leaving home and the twenty-five-year school land lease was expiring at the end of 1949. So it seemed that it was time to move on to a less demanding life with more modern living conditions. They tentatively decided they would sell out in the fall of 1949.

9. THE BLIZZARD OF 1949

T rue to form, the Sandhills would not let go of Mom and Dad without its own send off. On December 26, 1948, about 16 to 18 inches of snow fell. It was light and fluffy and easy to handle, but just a little late for Christmas. Most of the cattle were on the winter range, except for the cows that were going to have calves who were in the pasture south of the ranch. They were all on winter feed eating bunched hay and being fed "cotton cake," a supplement feed to help them get through the winter months.

January 1, 1949 was Sunday School day and it was being held at Min Johnston's home. Jim and Fern and their daughter, Sandra, were there for Christmas and Phyllis was teaching in the one room-schoolhouse. Bernie was feeding the cattle cotton cake. I was there, too, but that morning Ralph Munger gathered all the kids who were going to school in Curtis and drove them back to school. Everyone went to Sunday School.

Just after dinner and the services at Sunday School, a storm started. It came with very little warning. Everyone started for home. My folks made it back to the ranch, but it was tough going as the snow was blowing and the visibility was nearly zero. Some of the neighbors got stranded and some miraculously escaped death.

BERNIE

Bernie, who was there, remembers.

"We managed to get the chores done and took care of the livestock that were there. Jim and I tried to scout around the buildings and back of the barn, we found a few yearlings and two or three cows with small calves, that had drifted down from the north. We let them into the corral but nothing else could be done for the other cattle for the first three days of the raging blizzard.

"Thursday morning we awoke to a beautiful, calm day. The sun was shining. There wasn't a cloud in the ski nor a breath of wind.

"After chores and breakfast, Dad sent Jim

Pork and Sandy by turkey shed during the Blizzard of 1949.

and me to where we stored machinery to dig out an old horse-drawn sled that hadn't been used for several years. He figured with the snow so deep and having drifted into big mounds, the hay rack on wheels couldn't be used. We harnessed a team and got the sled out, rigged a box on it and started out to find the other cattle. We packed as much hay as we could get to stay on and started out to find the yearlings.

"We found them scattered all over in small bunches; some had drifted into a fence corner and about eight got trampled to death. We coaxed most of the rest home that day and got them into the corral where they had feed and water.

"On Friday, Jim and I went out by horseback and rounded up the rest of the yearlings and got them home in the corral. Dad saddled Rex, his favorite horse, and set out trying to find the cows in the south pasture. He found them behind a hill, completely drifted in by snow. He was able to get the horse through and kept going back and forth until he had made a path for the cows to get out. He was able to coax them through and they followed him to the little buildings across the lake where they could be fed and watered.

"Also on that Friday, knowing that no one was home at the Ralph Munger ranch, Dad sent Jim and I over to survey the situation and see what we could do. We did a few chores we could see that needed to be done, fed a few cattle and horses that were in the corrals and returned home to continue the struggle of taking care of our own. Ralph did get home that day. They had gotten back as far as Ellsworth and he borrowed a horse and was able to ride home.

"Early on the following week, our neighbor, Jack Brennan, was skinning some cattle he lost in the blizzard and stuck a knife in his eye. He came to our house, asking for help to feed his calves and do his chores and for someone to stay with his wife and daughter while he went to Alliance to a doctor. I went to help them for two days. Jack rode to Ellsworth and took the train to Alliance.

"Several days passed, most of them were windy and very cold. Dad spent most of his time doing the chores while Jim and I spent all day just feeding the cattle. We managed to feed the yearlings one day and the cows the next. The wind and cold were an everyday occurrence. Most days the temperature never got above zero. Our hands, feet, and faces were always sore because of the frostbite. We usually had to scoop the snow away from the hay stacks so we could get the hayrack close enough to load it. The boys couldn't get to school and Dad decided they could set up a school in one of the upstairs bedrooms. We managed to get to the school and the equipment and they started the second half of the school year.

"One decent day, a group of neighbors to the north, including my brother, Vern, shoveled their way to Ellsworth to get the mail and much needed supplies. They brought some things and, especially, the mail to us. Now that the road had been broken through, Phyllis and I decided to go to Ellsworth the next day. Soon after we started, the wind began to blow and the snow started drifting. We got hopelessly stuck and ended up walking back home. That was very difficult because we couldn't see. I remember Phyllis got quite a bit of frostbite. When you first get frostbite, you don't notice it. She wasn't dressed

Pork, Sandy and Jack during the Blizzard of 1949.

as warmly as I was, but she thought she was all right until the frost started to come out. We were sure glad to get back home.

"A few days later, we were getting low on groceries and, of course, Mom was anxious for the mail. Dad, Jim and I decided to scoop our way to Ellsworth. We got there and loaded the pickup with supplies and started back. We got as far as our neighbors, the Donahoes, where the drive shaft was torn off the pickup. It was nearly dark and we had no choice but to spend the night with the Donahoes. The next morning after breakfast, Jim walked back to Ellsworth to see if anyone could help us home. I stayed and helped shovel them out so they could do their chores. Roy Graham came with his four-wheel drive jeep and got us home. Mom, Phyllis and the boys kept up with the chores the best they could, but they were sure glad to see us.

"The days dragged into weeks. The days were always too short to get everything done. We lived like that for seven weeks. The weather finally began to moderate and it started to melt some. Even that was a slow process. Late one night we heard the rumbling of the big road graders and caterpillars coming through. The government had sent them to help the people. They went through the sandhills, plowing snow away from buildings and the remaining hay stacks. It was really a great help.

"There was many families in the Sandhills and beyond who suffered more than we did. Several people died in Nebraska and Wyoming as a result of that raging storm. I'm sure the storm really convinced Mom and Dad that it was time to retire. The one thing that I was especially grateful for was that Jim got snowed in with us. He had planned to return to his trade school just after New Year's. He was a great help during this time."

***

In the spring of 1949, my sister, Phyllis, went to Idaho to visit our brother, Homer. There she met Art Girton. They were married that June in an outdoor ceremony in the front yard of the ranch house. It was a big ceremony with lots of family and neighbors in attendance. Through their lives, they raised five children.

The kids got the job of decorating their car. We not only decorated the car, but caught and killed a sand viper snake and curled it up on the floor over the transmission. We took off the rotor cap and took out the rotor. After awhile we gave in and admitted what we had done. Dad told us to put the rotor back in. We did, but we put it in crooked and when it turned over, the rotor cracked. After that it wouldn't start at all. Aunt Hazel's daughter, Mary Louise, had just gotten married and she and her new husband, Dean, were there. Because he was new to the family, we tried to blame him, but I don't think it worked. Dad was very unhappy because they had to take his car on their honeymoon.

That summer it was haying as usual, but Mom and Dad were going ahead with their plans to sell out and move on to an easier life. They bought a farmstead just west of Scottsbluff. My sister, Jean, lived in one just down the road from theirs. The farmstead was a fourteen-acre place, just big enough for Dad to have a few milk cows, pigs and chickens.

Mom and Dad sold the ranch land in October 1949 and auctioned off the cattle, hay and machinery that November. That was a big day. People came from miles away to the sale. I believe that people came because they knew all of Dad's things would be high quality, because that is how Dad raised the cattle and built the machinery. As usual, all the neighbor ladies brought food and there was gallons of coffee. The auctioneer was a friend of the family named Harold Steggs.

During the next few days after the sale, Mom and Dad loaded up the hay rack with the household goods and other items they wanted to take and, with the tractor pulling, moved to Scottsbluff onto the farmstead they had selected and settled into semi-retirement.

10. Semi-Retirement

Our farmstead sat on fourteen acres. There was a modern three-bedroom house with an inside bathroom and telephone service, something they never had before. They were finally getting rid of the outside privy which certainly must have felt like a whole new world to them.

The place had a small milk house, chicken pen and a pig pen. It had six acres of alfalfa land, enough to feed a few head of milk cows, and seven acres of pasture land for them to graze in. It was perfect, because it was enough to give Dad things to do and, with my sister, Jean, living close by and Duck in the area, they would be free to travel around.

Duck married Edna Pettis in 1950. During their lifetime, they raised three children; Edna had one child by a previous marriage.

I had graduated from high school in the spring of 1949 and spent the fall and winter working in Gibbon and on the neighboring ranches in the sandhills. There wasn't much work available around Scottsbluff and I was just hanging around Mom and Dad's. It was getting pretty old, pretty fast. The Korean War was raging and I knew I would be drafted soon. I went down to the unemployment office, but they didn't have any work. As I walked out of their office, I spotted an Army and Air Force recruiting office, so I went in and talked to them about enlisting. Because I wasn't quite 18, Mom and Dad would have to sign for me. I went home and talked to Mom about it. She didn't think it was a good idea at all. I guess she could remember what my brothers and the family went through during World War II. Dad came in from the fields and, when I told him about it, he thought it was a great idea. So I enlisted.

My brother, Bernie, married Lucille Iossi in 1950. During their marriage, they raised two children. They were later divorced

1956 Family Portrait: Standing from left, Rodney, Jim, Jean, Bernie, Lois, Helen, Duck and Vern. Seated from left, Homer, Catherine, Dad, Mom, Phyllis and Margaret. Front, Marjorie and Don.

and Bernie married Sharon Hamburger.

Mom and Dad did a considerable amount of traveling in the 1950's. In 1951 they still had Pork and Jack living with them, and that year they traveled to Montana to see Homer and to Idaho to see Phyllis. They then went to California to see our sisters living there and to leave Pork and Jack with their mother, Margaret.

I married Norma Bowers in 1953. I was stationed in Saratoga Springs, New York with the Air Force at the time I met Norma. We have five children.

Mom and Dad visited us first when we lived in Ballston Spa and then again when we were stationed in Biloxi, Mississippi. Bernie and his wife came with them the second time. The last time we were stationed back in Saratoga and living in Ballston Spa. That was a memorable trip. Dad always wanted to visit Washington, D.C. and had always had a keen interest in politics. Mom's brother, Uncle Charlie, lived in Washington. While they were visiting us, we took a trip to Washington. Uncle Charlie's son took us on a tour of the Capital, White House, Arlington National Cemetery and both the Washington and Lincoln Monuments. Later that night Dad, Norma, our son, Duane, and I went to see a Washington Senators baseball game. Dad was always interested in baseball. I was even able to catch a foul ball as a souvenir for my son. I shall always cherish that visit from Mom and Dad.

Sometime in the later part of the 1950's, Dad and Bernie decided they would buy a farm in Bridgeport, Nebraska. They sold the farmstead and moved to the new farm around 1958. It was a full size farm with some 160 acres of farm land. They still had milk cows and chickens, and Dad still had his pigs to raise.

My sister, Helen took, sick in 1958. She died in Hot Springs, South Dakota in early 1959. That was a terrible blow to Mom and Dad.

During the 1960's, they were still able to take some trips but they slowed down some. There was still lots of visits from the kids and our city cousins. They still had a pony named "Annie" for the kids to play on.

Dad started getting sick in 1968. We visited them in 1968 just prior to my going overseas to Thailand. I could see that he was very sick and beginning to fail. He died in January 1969. Being stationed in Thailand, I was notified to come home. Norma and I got to the hospital in Scottsbluff just ten minutes after he had died. I have always regretted that, however Mom said that he probably wouldn't have recognized me. We were all home and it was pretty congested at the farm house so I told Mom that we would return to Kansas to our kids and we would come back a week later to spend a week with her after everyone had left. We did return and it was good for her because the loneliness had just set in. I remember her saying that "they had lived together a very short fifty eight years." She asked me, at that time, if there was anything of Dad's that I wanted to remember him by. I said that I would like to have the pocket watch that he always carried in his bib overalls, tied with a leather shoe lace which he always used to give the small kids to chew on and play with. She gave it to me and I shall always have it to pass on to one of my grandchildren.

Mom moved to Alliance shortly after that and resided in a senior housing complex. She died in January 1973.

They are buried in a simple plot in the Alliance Cemetery.

Their marker reads, LINEBACK Ocia B. 1893-1973, Paul S. 1890-1969. May they rest in peace. They certainly deserve it.

Annie, the pony, with grandkids Trina and Trevor Girton.

In total count Mom and Dad had 52 grandchildren and 103 great grandchildren. Four of the grandchildren died during infancy. I am not certain about the number of great-great grandchildren. I will leave that up to those who work in Genealogy.

During the years since I left Nebraska, while in the service and in later years, I have returned to Nebraska on several occasions. On each trip I have always tried to get to the Sandhills for a visit. The latest was in 1994, when Norma, myself and two of our daughters and their families visited the Ranch. The man who bought the place from Dad, Bill Shrewsbury, showed us all a great time. He took us to the site of the original homestead and to where the one-room schoolhouse sat. To say the least, our kids and grandchildren were very impressed. With all its harshness, the Sandhills has a kind of serene beauty that you just never forget.

The harsh and primitive conditions of homesteading in the Sandhills of Nebraska was well known to those who went through it. A few made it and went on to prosper. Others failed for whatever reasons. There is an old saying (author unknown) that goes "only the fittest of the fit will survive." *Our Mom and Dad were just that.*

THE END

Notes...

Duck, Margaret, Uncle Dave, Junior and Bernice loaded up on Cricket.

Notes...

Cattle on the summer range.

Notes...

Mom (right) and Min, one
of her best friends.